The Catbird's Song

The Beautiful Changes and Other Poems

Ceremony and Other Poems

A Bestiary *(editor, with Alexander Calder)*

Molière's The Misanthrope *(translator)*

Things of This World

Poems 1943–1956

Candide *(with Lillian Hellman)*

Poe: Complete Poems *(editor)*

Advice to a Prophet and Other Poems

Molière's Tartuffe *(translator)*

The Poems of Richard Wilbur

Loudmouse *(for children)*

Shakespeare: Poems *(co-editor, with Alfred Harbage)*

Walking to Sleep: New Poems and Translations

Molière's The School for Wives *(translator)*

Opposites

The Mind-Reader: New Poems

Responses: Prose Pieces, 1953–1976

Molière's The Learned Ladies *(translator)*

Racine's Andromache *(translator)*

Racine's Phaedra *(translator)*

New and Collected Poems

More Opposites

Molière's The School for Husbands and
Sganarelle, or The Imaginary Cuckold *(translator)*

Molière's Amphitryon

Richard Wilbur

The Catbird's Song

Prose Pieces 1963-1995

Harcourt Brace & Company

New York   San Diego   London

Requests for permission to make copies of any part of the work should
be mailed to: Permissions Department, Harcourt Brace & Company,
6277 Sea Harbor Drive, Orlando, Florida 32887-6777.

"Some Notes on 'Lying' " first appeared in Singular Voices: American
Poetry Today, Stephen Berg, editor (Avon Books, 1985).

Permissions acknowledgments appear on page xiii.

Library of Congress Cataloging-in-Publication Data
Wilbur, Richard, 1921–
The catbird's song : prose pieces. 1963–1995 / Richard Wilbur.—
1st ed.
p.   cm.
ISBN 0-15-100254-1
I. Title.
PS3545.I32165C38   1997
818'.5208—DC20   96-36229
CIP

Text set in Fairfield Medium
Designed by Camilla Filancia

Printed in the United States of America
First edition   A B C D E

FOR CHARLEE

Contents

Preface

BACK IN 1976, I brought out a first book of "prose by-products of a poet's life," and gave it the title of *Responses*. I called those by-products "responses" because, though every one of them had been something I wanted to write, none of them had been quite so gratuitous and unsolicited as a poem generally is. Indeed, in every case the piece had been something I was invited, or requested, or expected to do. This present gathering of prose is of the same responsive character.

The reader should be warned that this is not a collection of essays but a mixture or jumble of efforts in various other modes: the symposium statement, the anecdotal letter, the review, the short speech of welcome, the explication, and so on. There are certain forms which, unlike the essay, are pledged from the start to advocacy or praise: the foreword to someone else's book, for example, or the memorial tribute, of which there are several here. Though the discussion of "Poe and the Art of Suggestion" is hardly arcane, one can sometimes tell that it was composed not as an essay for the general reader, but as a paper to be read to a roomful of Poe scholars. It may seem that my words about Milton's companion poems are too brief, if considered as an essay; but in an Oscar Williams anthology of great poems, with small adjoining commentaries by various hands, their function was to introduce "L'Allegro" and "Il Penseroso" and not to up-stage them. Length is more reprehensible than brevity, of course, and I have put a long piece about the nearly forgotten poet Witter Bynner at the end of this book, where it will be reached only by readers of proven stamina. Long though it may seem in the present context, it was done as the introduction to a *Selected Poems,* and as such was committed to tracing the whole trajectory of an interesting career. From all these writings, with their different genera and occasions, I hope that something like a single voice transpires.

Since the 1976 *Responses,* which included the introductions I had written for three of my Molière translations, I have translated (and introduced) four more verse plays of Molière, as well as the *Phaedra* and *Andromache* of Racine. In deciding not to collect these six latter introductions here, I was encouraged by the fact that all of them, and their plays, are readily available and in print.

My thanks to all those at whose instance these jobs of writing were undertaken; and my particular gratitude to David Ferry and David Sofield, two friends who were so good as to read the whole manuscript.

R.W.

Key West, 1995

Norbert Krapf invited me to contribute to Under Open
Sky (1986), *a volume of appreciations of William Cullen
Bryant by a number of contemporary poets.*

A Word
from Cummington

THERE ARE in Cummington (population 600-odd) a few his-
torically-minded people who know of that Bryant who, during
his half-century of journalism in New York, was a militant ad-
vocate of the right to strike, a strong voice against slavery, a
furtherer of the arts, a force behind the planning of Central
Park, and the proprietor of a semi-rural retreat in Roslyn. But
for the most part in Cummington we think of him (somewhat
vaguely) as America's first eminent poet, and as an admirable
man who, first and last, had much to do with the town. There
is a marker on the site of his birthplace, near the Dawes Cem-
etery. The house in which he grew up, and which in his latter
years he purchased and enlarged for summer use—raising the
structure on jacks and constructing a new first floor beneath
it—is now a cultural landmark administered by the Trustees of
Reservations. Downhill from the Homestead is a ravine which
was never cleared, as the better part of Cummington was in his
boyhood, because it was too rugged and steep to be useful; its
acres of giant timber, still standing, must have predisposed the
young Bryant to become a poet of "wild nature" and an enthu-
siast of natural sublimities in painting. I hear that a newly made
path gives access to the area, and I am glad of the fact, because
I have never beaten my way into that forest without being much
bloodied by brambles; it would please Bryant, too, who wrote

some of his best lines on the subject of path-making. Cummington is grateful for the stone library which Bryant gave to the town in 1872, for the several thousand books with which he stocked it, and for the librarian's house which he built nearby; he also gave the land, and much of the money, for a long-used Bryant Schoolhouse.

He is our great man, and one or more of his poems is likely to be read aloud on any of our ceremonial occasions. Yet I suppose that as a personality he somewhat escapes our imaginations. To be sure, the visitor to the Homestead may come near him by responding to his delicate drawings of the local flora; and the chinning bar in the closet of his bedroom, over which the aged man repeatedly hoisted his beard each morning, may recall his reputation as a vigorous person and a strenuous hiker. What estranges him from us is the tone of many of his poems —sonorous, grave, noble, edifying, oratorically ruminative. What we miss in him, a fair bit of the time, is what we find (to make an outrageous contrast) in John Donne. In Donne, we hear a complex man talking, whereas Bryant sometimes sounds like a statue. Concentrating on a fluent orotundity, Bryant's poems too often lack the spontaneous figure, the surprisingly accurate word. Nor does one feel, as often as one would like to, that the world of which he speaks offers much resistance to the flow of his speech—that it has a life of its own. In "Inscription for the Entrance to a Wood," we meet "the squirrel, with raised paws erect," and cannot believe that he will ever move: he is a generic and illustrative squirrel, a step in a melodious argument and not a critter. Later, the "trunks of prostrate trees," because the poet is contending that unfallen Nature is glad, are obliged to "breathe fixed tranquillity." I am prepared to be persuaded of the goodness of all Nature, or of all things, but I would like to see some struggle toward that conclusion, some admission of contrary evidence, as in Whitman's "Song of Myself." Bryant's poem simply imposes the notion on its data—though it must be granted that the beautiful closing lines about the wind, because they allow the wind some initiative and because its behavior is plausible, go far toward saving the day.

"Thanatopsis," which my father took pleasure in declaiming over the shaving-bowl, is another poem in which elevation of style masks from the reader and from the poet the insufficiency of its argument. Underlying the poem, undoubtedly, is a Deistic persuasion that God made Nature, and that all things natural, including death, must therefore be all right. But the poem does not coherently say that. It tells us, rather gloomily, that in death we shall be reduced to the elements, losing our "individual being." It then gives us some sort of countermovement, wherein it is said that in death one has the company of the great of the past, and indeed of the whole of the dead, Earth being "the great tomb of man." This magnification of one's dust neither fortifies nor consoles; number and space and duration and "majesty" are simply laid on as a rhetorical enhancement. The closing section then confuses matters by describing physical dissolution, which is not mysterious, as an entry into a "mysterious realm," and urges an "unfaltering trust" in something unspecified. The effect of this is to give an air of bad faith or two-mindedness to the poem's biblical echoes and its suggestions of individual persistence ("sleep," "rest," "pleasant dreams.")

I have put off some of my Cummington friends by doubting the merits of "Thanatopsis," but fortunately it is possible to be two-minded about Bryant, who did after all write some truly superior poems. The yellow violet, which I had never seen before moving to the Berkshires, is strewn along all of our timber-trails in spring, and it seems to me that Bryant's well-known poem of that title does the flower double justice. In the first place, the yellow violet is exactly and gracefully described as to the shape and coloration of its blossom, the attitude of the blossom upon the stem, its fragrance, its time of emergence, its association with "the last year's leaves" or "the snow-bank's edges cold." At the same time, without any slighting of the object or any air of exploitation, the plant is made symbolic in two ways at once: such words as "Modest," "peeps," "faint" and "Virgin" work toward one effect, while the ideas of hardiness and sun-brightness in stanzas 3–4 produce another. The result is an emblem of modest excellence so artfully arrived at that a comparatively unforced transition to one of "Nature's teachings" may be made in the seventh stanza.

To speak of yet another famous poem, "To a Waterfowl" strikes me as moving from description to moral with complete success. It is a poem which opens with a question—which inquires as well as asserts or teaches. One of its strengths is that it implicitly admits the possibility of lostness and unbelief and wearily giving up; it proceeds from rosy light to darkness, from the known to the unknown; there are sinister overtones in such words as "solitary," "desert," and "abyss." All of this keeps the poem honest and strengthens its affirmation. The bird and its progress are realized in a fresh, simple, economical language which Bryant tends to lose when he expatiates in enjambed pentameters. There is a fine concreteness in such words as "chafed" and "fanned," a plain eloquence in "Lone wandering, but not lost," and the word "scream" (line 23) brilliantly crowns a description in which the waterfowl is not an illustration but a living fact. There are many more things to praise here, but I shall mention just one: the way that deep calls to deep in this poem, as the "rosy depths" of line 3 are echoed in the "deeply" of line 27, thus further weaving the moral into the experience. I suppose, if there must be rankings and priorities, that "To a Waterfowl" may be America's first flawless poem.

TO A WATERFOWL

Whither, midst falling dew,
While glow the heavens with the last steps of day,
Far, through their rosy depths, dost thou pursue
Thy solitary way?

Vainly the fowler's eye
Might mark thy distant flight to do thee wrong,
As, darkly painted on the crimson sky,
Thy figure floats along.

Seek'st thou the plashy brink
Of weedy lake, or marge of river wide,
Or where the rocking billows rise and sink
On the chafed ocean-side?

There is a Power whose care
Teaches thy way along that pathless coast—
The desert and illimitable air—
Lone wandering, but not lost.

All day thy wings have fanned,
At that far height, the cold, thin atmosphere,
Yet stoop not, weary, to the welcome land,
Though the dark night is near.

And soon that toil shall end;
Soon shalt thou find a summer home, and rest,
And scream among thy fellows; reeds shall bend,
Soon, o'er thy sheltered nest.

Thou'rt gone, the abyss of heaven
Hath swallowed up thy form; yet, on my heart
Deeply has sunk the lesson thou hast given,
And shall not soon depart.

He who, from zone to zone,
Guides through the boundless sky thy certain flight,
In the long way that I must tread alone,
Will lead my steps aright.

At Kent Ljungquist's and Ben Fisher's invitation, I read this paper to the Poe Studies Association during the MLA convention of 1981. Though my opinion of Julian Symons's book on Poe is unchanged, I have lately discovered that he is a crack mystery writer.

Poe and the Art of Suggestion

POE WELL UNDERSTOOD that people of a strongly prosaic turn of mind are often drawn to mystic or imaginative literature, which they read with a fascinated resistance. The initially skeptical narrator of "MS. Found in a Bottle" has long enjoyed the German moralists, "not," he says, "from any ill-advised admiration of their eloquent madness, but from the ease with which my habits of rigid thought enabled me to detect their falsities." And the hero of "Berenice," once his visionary disposition has been destroyed by disease, is attracted to St. Augustine's *City of God* because of what he calls its "imaginative and inconsequential nature." Some scholars seem to approach Poe himself in a similar spirit of charmed mistrust, confining their often valuable studies to matters of fact, or apparent fact, while resisting Poe's repeated advice that imaginative writing be searched for undercurrents of meaning.

One recent resister of Poe is Julian Symons, whose book *The Tell-Tale Heart* asserts, among other things, that while "William Wilson" is "absolutely clear" as symbolic fiction, Poe's work in general is intrinsically vague and incapable of interpretation. Though I hesitate to agree with Mr. Symons about anything, I think him correct in saying that "Wilson" is one of the few fictions in Poe which have the suggestive clarity of a Hawthorne story. We must be grateful that we have, in "Wilson," a common ground on which all readers of Poe may meet—a story which plainly concerns the gradual division of a once harmonious soul into warring faculties; which embodies the conflict between the degraded will and the moral sense in the persons of Wilson and his double; which involves not only earth but Heaven and Hell; and which ends in spiritual death. Where I differ with Mr. Symons is in his inclination to dismiss as insoluble anything less perspicuous than "William Wilson." "Wilson" may be atypical in its clarity, but it is typical of Poe in its concerns, in its images and locutions, in its first-person narration, and in its symbolic or allegorical method. The thing to do, I think, is to push off from "Wilson" into the *mare tenebrarum* of the other works—seeing, for example, whether the high and low voices of the two Wilsons may help one to understand the variable registers of Roderick Usher, or of Dupin, or whether it is significant that the mummer who represents the Red Death moves with a step "solemn and measured," like Dr. Bransby in "William Wilson" or the figure of Conscience in *Politian*. Because Poe's machinery of suggestion can be submerged and sly, such a quest must involve confusion and error, but at least it will have the virtue of responding to what is there.

We all know how slow a work of Poe's may be to release its meaning. I have been reading "Israfel," on and off, for most of my life, and I have always regarded it as a simple, flawed, and occasionally felicitous piece in which an earthly poet, while not apologizing for his own limited efforts, applauds the superior lyric powers of an angel. I still read the poem in the same general way, but not long ago I was made suddenly aware that the poem is subtler and more argumentative than I had thought, and that it may be taken, from beginning to end, as a treatise on the place of passion in poetry. Poe's poetic theory, which reached its full development in "The Poetic Principle," distinguishes as we know three primary divisions of the "world of mind": the intellect, which pursues truth; taste, which has for its object beauty; and the moral sense, which concerns itself with duty. Poetry being a wild effort to capture supernal beauty, it is the province of taste alone. The intellect and the moral sense, with its mundane didacticism, are inimical to poetry, and are admissible in a poem only if utterly subjected to the purposes of taste. Since poetry aims at "an elevating excitement of the soul," a spiritual or Uranian kind of love may be the truest of poetic themes; but as for passion, which is "an intoxication of the heart," Poe agrees with Coleridge that it degrades the soul and is discordant with poetry.

And yet, in "Israfel," we meet an angel whose very instrument is the heart, and whose song is all fire, fervor, and "burning measures." He causes the stars to be giddy, the enamored moon to totter and blush, the lightning to be red, and all of his celestial hearers to be mute with rapture. Why is Israfel's song not a degrading performance? We know that it cannot be, since the stars suspend their hymns to God in order to hear it. Most of the answers, however, are given by condensed and muffled implication in the fourth stanza:

> But the skies that angel trod,
>   Where deep thoughts are a duty—
>   Where Love's a grown-up God—
>   Where the Houri glances are
>   Imbued with all the beauty
>   Which we worship in a star.

Israfel's condition in heaven is here described in terms of the triad of faculties which I have just mentioned. *Deep thoughts* have to do with the intellect, *duty* pertains to the moral sense, and *beauty* to the aesthetic sense, or taste. An angelic soul, it seems, has the same constituents as a human soul, but the difference is that Israfel is an inhabitant of the skies. Throughout his early work, from "Al Aaraaf" onward, Poe argues that intellectual knowledge is not fit for man in the earthly condition of his soul, and that it wars with that sense of beauty which is our sole means of approaching the divine; but for the angel Israfel, who dwells "in the high Heaven of pure knowledge," there is no conflict between intellect and taste, and these faculties are in turn perfectly attuned to the moral sense. Israfel has an intact and harmonious soul, as the poet of Earth does not.

Often, when Poe wishes to evoke supernal beauty, he will do so by combining erotic words or images with inhibitory ideas. When Nesace, the spirit of Beauty, arrives at her palace in the second part of "Al Aaraaf," we are given this picture: "From the wild energy of wanton haste/ Her cheeks were flushing and her lips apart;/ The zone that clung about her gentle waist/ Had burst beneath the heaving of her heart." Wantonness, flushing, parted lips and a burst zone are all very libidinous, but these effects are countered by the fact that she is a heavenly spirit whom we have just seen praying to God, and that she is here frozen into immobility like a statue—a statue perhaps by Canova, that sculptor whom Mario Praz once aptly dubbed "The Erotic Refrigerator." The same effect of chastened passion is achieved in two words in the poem "Evening Star," where Poe extols the "distant fire" of Venus. The dark-eyed Houri glances in "Israfel" may for a moment suggest mere voluptuousness, but then we are told that they are "Imbued with all the beauty/

Which we worship in a star"—that they are objects of distanced and spiritual devotion. Having chastened his Houris, Poe can then proceed in his following lines to Q.E.D.: "Therefore, thou are not wrong,/ Israfeli, who despisest/ An unimpassioned song. . . ." Owing to his psychic wholeness and his heavenly environment, Israfel's song can be both passionate and pure; he can handle the erotic; he can intoxicate his heart without risking his spiritual balance; whereas the poet of Earth, a divided soul in a degraded environment, must forever be wary of falling into "The napthalene river of passion accurst."

The first version of "Israfel" is even more concentrated on the theme of passion in poetry than the later and more familiar one, but the second contains a parenthetical addition which once seemed to me decorative at best, but now strikes me as thoroughly pertinent. I refer to the lines in which we are told how "the red levin/ (With the rapid Pleiads even,/ Which were seven,)/ Pauses in Heaven." The Pleiades are rapid because, when they were nymphs on Earth, they were pursued by the enamored hunter Orion; translated to Heaven by Zeus, they are safe from Orion's lust, but are still in an attitude of flight from him. As for the reduction of their number from seven to six, one of the Pleiades (named Merope) forsook the skies, according to Ovid, because of her passion for a mortal. Poe's evocation of the Pleiades is thus a double proof that, in Israfel's poetic preserve, unruly earthly passion is not allowed. The fall of Merope resembles, of course, the fall of Angelo and Ianthe in "Al Aaraaf," and means exactly the same thing. Let me add, incidentally, that Merope's fall is a felicitous touch because it affords a countermovement to the upward yearning of the speaker of the poem.

Assuming that all these things are in "Israfel," why did it

take me so long to see them? For one thing, Poe is theoretically opposed to *thinking* in poetry, and there are very few of his poems—the sonnet to Mrs. Clemm would be one of them—which are forthrightly argumentative in nature. One does not therefore feel encouraged to read "Israfel" as an implicit discourse on the facultative and emotional basis of poetry in Heaven and Earth. On the contrary, a poem which offers the rhymes *wrong, song, belong* and *long* within a six-line stanza, and gives us *levin, even, seven* and *Heaven* in successive lines, seems chiefly musical rather than verbal in intention—a melodic tribute to the angel's song. The impression that music has priority is strengthened when one notes that, in a present-tense poem, the verb *tread* has been wrenched into the past tense so as to rhyme with *God*. Though there are handsome passages in "Israfel," some of the language seems thoughtless or casual. When Poe seeks to broaden the range of Israfel's passion by speaking of "Thy grief, thy joy, thy hate, thy love," he slips into nonsense; an angel who dwells in "perfect bliss" does not sing of grief and hate. To describe the instrumental use of heart-strings as "unusual" is bathetic, to say the least. In what I take to be the crucial stanza, the expression "deep thoughts" may sound too banal to be taken seriously, while "duty" and "beauty," though they intend to say a great deal, may in so musical a poem be passed over as mere facile rhyming. Finally, although Poe the critic contended that "every work of art should contain within itself all that is requisite for its own comprehension," "Israfel" does not, in my experience, yield all of its suggested ideas unless one brings a general familiarity with Poe to bear on it.

Some time ago, at a funeral, I heard a familiar passage from St. Paul and had a delayed insight into "Annabel Lee." I had meant to electrify you with the quotation tonight, but in preparing to write this paper I found that the passage is already cited in Professor Mabbott's notes to the poem. This gave me mixed feelings of disappointment and comfort; as Allen Tate once remarked, in interpreting Poe we often fear that we are mad, and it can be reassuring to find that one is not being wholly original. So far as I know, the implications of the passage in question have not been explored, and so I shall state them briefly. Poe's poem says that Annabel Lee and her lover are children, and are therefore close to heaven and unsullied by the world. Their love is "more than love"; it is not merely a strong affection but a kind of blessed communion which the very angels might wish to enjoy. Thus far, what we have is a restatement, in one of Poe's last poems, of some lines from "Tamerlane": "Love—as in infancy was mine—/ 'Twas such as angel minds above/ Might envy...." But now Poe turns that hyperbole into narrative, and most improbably has the envious angels cause the death of Annabel Lee; with whom, nonetheless, the lover continues somehow to be in unbroken communion: "And neither the angels in Heaven above/ Nor the demons down under the sea/ Can ever dissever my soul from the soul/ Of the beautiful ANNABEL LEE...." One of the lessons in the Episcopal *Order for the Burial of the Dead* is taken from the eighth chapter of St. Paul's *Epistle to the Romans*. I shall read to you only the words which are applicable here: "For I am persuaded, that neither death, nor life, nor angels, nor principalities, nor powers, nor things present, nor things to come, nor height, nor depth, nor any other creature, shall be able to separate us from the love of God...." It seems clear to me that St. Paul has emboldened Poe to imagine his angels as seeking to separate love from love and man from God, and that Poe's adaptation of the passage from *Romans* has the inescapable effect of identifying Annabel Lee with "the love of God." Within the burial rite, St. Paul's words are a promise that the dead are safely united with their Maker; but the passage as used by Poe asserts that the soul of Annabel's lover shall never be severed from hers, or from the divine love and beauty which her soul communicates. Annabel Lee, then, is not only a kinswoman of the angels, but a mediatory spirit like Nesace or the Lady Ligeia. Her story, in fact, is the Ligeia story without Rowena. In "Annabel Lee," the angelic mediatrix is physically lost, but never is she lost to her lover's spirit, which nightly communes with her soul and its message through the glory of the moon and the divine beauty and order of the stars.

If I ask why an Episcopalian took so long to find St. Paul in "Annabel Lee," the answer is once again in good part a matter of tone, or music. The poem might be described as the balladic heightened into the vatic. It begins with the language and movement of ballad—"It was many and many a year ago"—but instead of regular stanzas, a consecutive story, a refrain, and the expected variations of rhyme, we have a changeable stanza, elaborate and irregular repetitions, and a rapt, chanting insistence on such rhymes as *sea, Lee, me,* and *we.* The poem's rich sound, exultant anapests, and vatic repetitions assimilate everything to one powerful effect, salvaging all banalities about moonbeams and dreams, and quite overwhelming the accents of St. Paul. For someone of my generation, to think of the use of quotations in poetry is to think of T. S. Eliot and his *Waste Land.* Despite the fact that more than ten percent of Eliot's poem consists of echoes, and despite the continual irruption of various dramatic voices, there is at all times a recognizable ground voice, which is the voice of the poet. We know when

Eliot is talking, and when we are hearing the Buddha. But the voice of Poe's poem does not yield the floor to any other, and if after many readings one notices a smothered reference to Romans: 8, one does not even then feel strongly prompted, as one would in Eliot, to ponder the logic of the allusion.

There are similar obstacles, in Poe's tales, to the taking of his suggested meaning, though this is not true of them all. It seems to me that the choice of the name Prospero, in "The Masque of the Red Death," is both brilliant and accessible; Poe's Prospero resembles Shakespeare's in that he is separated from his dominions, but a more important resemblance is that both are capable of summoning up imaginary revels. The name Prospero thus readies us to see what the tale makes plain, that the Prince's thousand companions are all creatures of dream. In writing "The Tell-Tale Heart," a year after "The Masque of the Red Death," Poe was again thinking of Shakespeare, and when a ray of the mad hero's dark-lantern is directed at the old man's vulture eye, falling precisely upon "the damned spot," few readers would fail to think of *Macbeth*. Yet in my experience, this echo does not work so promptly as the reference to Prospero, and may not even be entertained, by the reader, as a suggestion. I think this occurs in part because "The Masque of the Red Death" is told in a deliberate authorial voice capable of firm intimations, whereas "The Tell-Tale Heart" is the first-person narrative of a terror-prone madman who is breathless with the desire to boast of his cleverness, and also to confess. His choppy, nervous, repetitive and self-obsessed language is in itself superbly suggestive of a state of mind, but it is not a likely fabric in which to detect ponderable literary allusions.

Yet they are present. Hearing a small sound, Poe's old man springs up in bed and cries "Who's there?," which is also the cry of Macbeth in Duncan's bedchamber, hearing a spectral voice. Poe's narrator then tells how the old man, "ever since the first slight noise," has been lying awake and saying to himself: "It is nothing but the wind in the chimney—it is only a mouse crossing the floor . . . it is only a cricket which has made a single chirp." Macbeth, descending from Duncan's chamber, asks: "Didst thou not hear a noise?" and his wife replies: "I heard the owl scream and the cricket cry." When Lady Macbeth says "Out, damned spot," she is washing her hands of imaginary blood, and Poe takes up the idea again when he has his narrator say, while burying his dismembered victim beneath the floorboards: "There was nothing to wash out—no stain of any kind —no blood-spot whatever." The madman's victim is referred to, throughout the story, simply as "the old man," and that may put one in mind of Lady Macbeth's saying: "Yet who would have thought the old man to have had so much blood in him?" In addition to such echoes faint or strong, there are patent resemblances in Poe's tale to the plot of *Macbeth:* we have the nocturnal murder of an old man in his bedchamber, we have a knocking at the gate (or the street door, if you will), and, as in the matter of Banquo's ghost, we have a killer unhinged by hallucinations of his victim. All of this, nevertheless, is very slow to transpire, because it is largely screened by the narration and also, I suspect, because one may not at once divine its reason for being there.

Why does Poe introduce an undercurrent of *Macbeth* into his story? I think it is because, in his accounts of psychic division, Poe often conceived inner conflicts in terms of regicide, rebellion, or usurpation. Tamerlane says: "My passions, from that hapless hour/ Usurp'd a tyranny. . . ." William Wilson murderously rebels against the "inscrutable tyranny" of his conscience; in "The Haunted Palace," a ruler called "the monarch Thought" is dethroned in a palace revolution. If we take this indication—and there are many others—that on some level the killer and victim of "The Tell-Tale Heart" are one person, that they have one heart and one riven nature, what names shall we assign to these portions of a self? The old man's offending eye may be helpful: for one thing, it is a "pale blue eye, with a film over it." We know, from "The Man of the Crowd," that "when the film from the mental vision departs," a condition of preternatural insight ensues. It follows that a filmy eye like the old man's represents a cramped, mundane and unimaginative awareness of things, as opposed to that of the narrator, who can hear all things in heaven, earth, and hell. That the old man's eye is like that of a vulture, and that his look makes the narrator's blood run cold, must remind one further of the "Sonnet—To Science"; there the scientific spirit, which is likened to destroying time, alters all with its peering eyes, preys like a vulture upon the poet's heart, and turns all to "dull realities."

Given Poe's insistence, in "The Tell-Tale Heart," on time and heart and vulture eye, I take it for a dead certainty that the story is consciously recalling the "Sonnet—To Science." Did Poe expect his reader to do the same? I doubt it very much. Even when Poe was contemplating unified collections, as in the days of the Folio Club project, I see no evidence that he meant his reader to elucidate one poem or story by reference to another. Yet for us, as we struggle to understand him, cross-reference is an indispensable tool, and that is one measure of his difficulty. When the hero of "The Pit and the Pendulum" swoons, the voices of his inquisitors merge into a "dreamy indeterminate hum" suggestive of "the burr of a mill-wheel." If we apply that to the

Simoom of "MS. Found in a Bottle," which the narrator first hears as "a loud humming noise" like that caused by "the rapid revolution of a mill-wheel," we are confirmed in our sense that the narrator is swooning, that his mind is embarking on a dream. The devil, in "Bon-Bon," takes off his green spectacles and reveals that he has no eyes; his vision, he explains, is of the soul, and includes the power to read the thoughts of any creature. In "The Purloined Letter" and "The Mystery of Marie Roget," Dupin, too, wears green spectacles which, whatever their practical uses as camouflage, serve also to symbolize the fact that he, like the devil, is a mind reader and a seer. But not all similarities in Poe signify the same thing. To return to the "Sonnet—To Science" and "The Tell-Tale Heart," the poem is strong in its advocacy of the oppressed and rebellious poet, and of his effort to "seek for beauty in some happier star." In "The Tell-Tale Heart," however, what we have is not advocacy of the afflicted imagination but a description of its predicament: the story seems to say that, if imagination rebels against everyday temporal consciousness and earthly attachments, the cost may be a self-destructive madness. Let me offer another example of dissimilar similarity. Poe's Monos and Una withdraw from the "infected" and "diseased" world about them and "wrap their spirits in dreams"; Prince Prospero, in a story written several months later, withdraws into *his* dreams from a world devastated by Pestilence. The situations sound identical, but they are not, and the difference is plain from the characters of the dreams in question. The mood in which Prospero forsakes the world is described by Poe in two brutal sentences: "The external world could take care of itself. In the meantime, it was folly to grieve, or to think." Prince Prospero thus fatally fragments himself: he does not subordinate his intellect to imagination, but attempts to nullify it; and as for the moral sense, which might move him to grieve for his abandoned subjects, he defies it just as William Wilson did, and with the same suicidal consequences. The dreams which his "guiding taste" creates, though in some respects they resemble happier visions elsewhere in Poe, are far from being aspirant and spiritual—they are, in fact, a kind of "freaking out," and Poe is at pains to tell us that they partake of the mad, the terrible, and the disgusting. Monos and Una, confronted likewise by the corruption of our planet and the running-out of earthly time, engage not in desperate fantasy but in eager visions of an Earth purified by fire and of a regenerate mankind in whom taste and intellect shall be reconciled once more. Their very different dreams have a different and heavenly issue.

Though Poe did not write one thing to explain another, and though similarities may deceive, certain tales do give us particularly clear and trustworthy keys to Poe's suggestive methods. It is not only "William Wilson" which lets us get a foot in the door. In "The Island of the Fay," we are made witnesses to the process by which deepening reverie may transform a landscape into a mirror of the psyche—changing the water-borne flakes of sycamore bark, for example, into the flickering images of the hypnagogic state; this demonstration of the interiorizing of nature can make it easier for us to enter and navigate the psychic scenery of such a piece as "The Domain of Arnheim." "The Pit and the Pendulum," by commencing with a cataract of apocalyptic echoes from scripture, gives fair warning that it is going to be two stories at once—the literal story of a tortured prisoner and the symbolic story of a soul in danger of damnation on Judgment Day. Therefore the narrative is full of expressions, like "deliverance," "hope," "despair," and "eternal night," which at once belong to a description of tormented captivity and by their overtones imply another tale in which a terrified spirit awaits God's final justice or mercy. This obvious and brilliant use of resonant words, in "The Pit and the Pendulum," helps one to recognize similar effects elsewhere—in "The Fall of the House of Usher," for example, where such a word as "trepidation" not only conveys the fear and trembling and tension which pervade Roderick's domain, but hints also that the very cosmos is falling into disorder and will soon collapse toward its original state of unity. "Ligeia" is a rich and difficult story, yet for the common reader it is a relatively clear introduction to Poe's use of alchemical symbolism. Ligeia's presence is golden, her absence is leaden, and what happens to Rowena is a transmutation. In order to register these things, the common reader need know no more of alchemy than he could get from Milton's "Il Penseroso," whose Goddess Melancholy is described in terms of gold and lead, and who, like the Lady Ligeia, sponsors the transmutation of earthly experience into spiritual knowledge. If he grasps this aspect of "Ligeia" by way of Milton, as was the case with me, the common reader may then be able to sense something of the more complex alchemical goings-on in Roderick Usher's house.

But now I arrive at the necessity of granting that Poe is an odd sort of symbolic writer who often enshrouds his mystic meanings as if they were secret doctrine, and who is given to puzzle-making and teasing. No amount of "Il Penseroso" will help us to dig up all the alchemical treasure of "The Gold Bug"; for that, we must either become hermetic adepts or consult Professor St. Armand's authoritative essay. Often, Poe will challenge or mystify us by cloaking his hints in an ancient or foreign language: to be quite certain that the comic tales "Loss of

Breath" and "Bon-Bon" have serious implications of an anti-physical or antimaterialist nature, the reader must absorb a Latin footnote and a Greek pun. I have already noted elsewhere that in "The Murders in the Rue Morgue" Poe uses the French phrase *au troisième* as one indication that Dupin's fourth-floor apartment, and that of the murdered women, are in some ulterior sense the same dwelling. Let me mention another bit of linguistic coyness from the same story. As the narrator and Dupin walk home from inspecting the scene of the crime, we are given this strange sentence: "I have said that the whims of my friend were manifold, and that *Je les ménageais*—for this phrase there is no English equivalent." That is complete bunk, of course; Poe uses the same verb *ménager* as a past participle in "The System of Doctor Tarr and Professor Fether," and promptly translates it as "humored." Here, the supposedly untranslatable phrase means simply that the narrator humored Dupin, or fell in with his whims. Why should Poe seek to make a mystery of the word *ménager*? My guess is that he wants us to contemplate the word, and in the process think of the closely related words *ménage* and *ménagerie*; that he wants us to realize, with the aid of other promptings, that there are three similar *ménages* in the story—each secluded, each with two occupants—and that one of these households, because it contains an orangoutang, is also a menagerie. To arrive at those perceptions is to be on one's way perhaps to detecting an occult level of the story at which (as I've proposed elsewhere) all the ménages are one, all of the occupants are principles of one nature, and the theme is the need to recognize and control the beast in oneself. If Poe's monkey business with the word *ménager* is meant to work in the way I have surmised, there may be a similar provocation in "The Fall of the House of Usher," when the valet who has answered the door is said to "usher" the narrator into the presence of Roderick. Poe is inviting us, I suspect, to brood upon "usher" both as word and as name. It has been noticed that the primary meaning of "usher" is "door-keeper," which accords with the valet's function in answering Roderick's door. The English word "usher" derives from *ostia-rius*, which is based upon *os*, the Latin word for mouth, and thus the word "usher" contains an etymological identification of door and mouth which is consonant with the architectural symbolism of the story. Another meaning of "usher," which we encounter in "William Wilson," is "assistant schoolmaster," and I suppose that Roderick might be seen as instructing the half-comprehending narrator in the mysteries of spiritual regeneration. But what most appeals to me—and I find that my notion is shared by Professor Earl Wilcox—is the possibility that the name "Usher" is meant to evoke the seventeenth-century Anglican archbishop James Ussher, whose chronology of the world, beginning with the creation in 4004 B.C., was to be found in many Bibles of Poe's day. Poe was well aware of Ussher's chronology, referring to it in several tales and in his preface to the projected *Tales of the Folio Club*. The action of "The Fall of the House of Usher" is the purification and reintegration of a soul, but in the background of the story is a similar development in the whole cosmos, a development which becomes explicit when the story's final sentence echoes *Revelation*'s prophecy of the fall of Babylon. In the light of the story's apocalyptic close, Poe's title "The Fall of the House of Usher" could mean not only the collapse of Roderick's house but the end of Bishop Ussher's chronology, the uncreation of the world.

None of these hunches about the word (or name) "usher" is capable of firm proof, so far as I can see; but it is certain that

Poe *provokes* us to such speculations, and not to attempt a response is not to read him fully. Let me now mention one more kind of teasing which we find in Poe—his use of absurdity and self-contradiction. In "The Purloined Letter," Dupin calls on the Minister D—, and finds him "at home, yawning, lounging, and dawdling, as usual, and pretending to be in the last extremity of ennui. He is"—Dupin goes on—"he is, perhaps, the most really energetic human being now alive—but that is only when nobody sees him." What Dupin says is preposterous, of course; how should he or anyone else know how the Minister D— looks and behaves when alone? Dupin could possess such knowledge only if he *were* the Minister D—. Well, perhaps he is. In the first half of "The Purloined Letter," Dupin and the Minister seem quite distinct characters, the only connections between them being that both are poets, that both have names beginning with D, and that Dupin knows something of the Minister's intellectual style and political leanings. In the second half of the story, however, the reader is more and more incited to merge his conceptions of Dupin and the Minister, and to perceive that they are "doubles." We are told that the Minister has a brother, who like him has literary gifts. Dupin belatedly acknowledges that he knows the Minister well. Both men, we find, are poetic geniuses with a consequent built-in mastery of mathematics, and Dupin, because of this identity of intellects, can unerringly read the Minister's thoughts. Both men are lynx-eyed, especially when it comes to observing letters; both know the trick of replacing one letter with another; it turns out that the Minister is "well acquainted" with Dupin's handwriting; it develops that the two men, who are now contending over the honor of a queen, have been rivals before, in Vienna; and in Dupin's concluding quotation from Crébillon, the reader is invited to liken Dupin and the Minister to the royal brothers Atreus and Thyestes, whose bloody feud began with Thyestes' seduction of Atreus' queen Aerope. This barrage of suggestion forces one to divine a "mystic" dimension of the story in which, as at the close of "William Wilson," the good and evil sides of one person are in conflict over a woman's honor and what it symbolizes. The absurdity to which I called your attention—Dupin's assertion that he knows what the Minister looks like "when nobody sees him"—is not, then, a slip of the pen but one brilliant and challenging hint in a narrative full of pokes and nudges.

As James Gargano and I once remarked in conversation, there are a number of other Poe tales in which initially discrete characters are made to converge, and to betray a relationship more intimate than was at first described. The narrator of "The Assignation" begins by claiming only a "slight acquaintance" with the visionary hero, but in the latter part of the story the hero is called "my friend," and there is considerable evidence that narrator and hero are close indeed. Similarly, the narrator of "The Fall of the House of Usher" says in his second paragraph that "many years have elapsed" since his last meeting with Roderick; but by the eighth paragraph, confronting Roderick in his *studio*, the narrator marvels that his host's appearance should have changed so greatly "in so brief a period." These absurdities or inconsistencies can be explained, but I shall not try to do so now; suffice it to say that they are not mistakes but deliberate contradictions, intended (I think) to jar us into an awareness that the narrator has passed from one state of consciousness into another.

I have now been out on a limb for quite a while, saying the sort of thing which would madden Mr. Julian Symons, and I think it is time for me to climb down and sum up. Drawing on my own wrestlings with Poe, I have given a few examples of what may happen if one treats him as a readable author whose meanings can sometimes be arrived at. I've mentioned some, but certainly not all, of Poe's modes of suggestion, and given examples of how cross-reference can both help and mislead the reader. I've tried to describe, in particular cases, some of the ways in which Poe's poems and stories can insulate us from their content and delay our discovery of things which, once discovered, seem obvious. Finally, I have conceded to Poe's detractors that he is the most secretive and difficult of our great symbolic writers. How much of him will permanently elude us, how much we can figure out, we can only learn by trying.

This review of Newton Arvin's Longfellow: His Life and
Work *appeared in the second issue of* The New York Review
of Books, *Spring 1963.*

Longfellow

AFTER HIS SECOND WIFE'S horrible death by fire, in 1861,
Longfellow's face was too seared to be shaven, and he grew a
beard. It was this beard in which he was received by Queen
Victoria, toasted by Gladstone, and seen by a vast international
public as the foremost of American poets. For those of us who
were taught in grade school to revere him and in college to
shrug him off, the beard is an obstacle to fresh acquaintance,
and Newton Arvin has wisely chosen a frontispiece in which the
forty-eight-year-old man is obscured only by burnsides. What
the photograph shows, immediately, is the "lit-up face and glow-
ing warmth and courtesy" which Whitman encountered. But
that we might have guessed: less expected is the general air of
robust youthfulness. In the lift of the head, in the strong brows
and nose, there is a look of romantic adventurousness, or per-
haps, as Mr. Arvin suggests, of command. The eyes are direct,
clear, and full of life, though a pronounced fold at the outer
corners gives them a touch of sadness. The mouth, in contra-
diction to all that may seem rugged in the other features, is
generous, comfort-loving, and a bit unformed.

Like the frontispiece, Mr. Arvin's excellent account of Long-
fellow's life presents the man rather than the idol. This is not
to say that the biographical chapters confer any illusion of in-
timacy with Longfellow; the proportions of the study permit very
little detail, very little quotation from journal or letters; the
method is neither dramatic nor atmospheric, and we do not

fancy that we are "there." We do, however, gain from Mr. Arvin's spare, pointed narrative a just perspective on a unique career, and an admirably reserved interpretation of a character which was less simple than it seemed.

Few writers have been so fortunate. Longfellow suffered three painful bereavements, but the rest of his life was incessantly sweet. He was born into a cultured, comfortable family of good standing, and brought up in a hometown—Portland, Maine—which he never ceased to love. As a senior at Bowdoin College he developed a fervent aspiration toward "future eminence in literature," and events promptly conspired to give him his wish. Bowdoin's trustees preserved him from the study of law by appointing him, at the age of eighteen, to a professorship of modern languages, and after three years of happy preparation abroad he returned to teach, first at Bowdoin, and then for eighteen years at Harvard. If he sometimes found teaching onerous, he was always successful at it, and never wearied of his material. As America's first poet-professor he was luckier than many since, in that for him there was "a complex and fruitful reaction between literary scholarship and literary creation." His house in Cambridge seemed to Emerson a palace; his domestic life, as Mr. Arvin says, "was one of almost pure felicity"; and his poetic reputation, beginning with *Voices of the Night* in 1839, grew steadily greater. He was translated, while living, into more than twenty languages, and on his death to the poets' corner of Westminster Abbey.

It was a lucky life, lived directly and serenely to its goal; and there were, as Mr. Arvin tells, other exceptional things about it. "Modern Languages" was not an established discipline in the 1820s, and Longfellow's teaching of European languages and literatures was thus a relatively fresh venture. He devised his own textbooks at Bowdoin; he was the first in America to offer a course in Goethe's *Faust;* his unprecedented collection of translations, *The Poets and Poetry of Europe,* was an enlightenment to all of literate America. In short, Longfellow's scholarly career had a creativeness which is now seldom remembered. Nor do we readily associate with Longfellow the unacademic gusto with which he approached his academic material: he learned his languages not in the schoolrooms and libraries of Europe, but in great measure by mixing in the daily life of people of all classes; his teaching was based on "the contagion of personal enthusiasm." Another aspect of the man was the way in which, as Henry James put it, "his 'European' culture and his native kept house together." Longfellow was, in his time, a major channel of European influence, and yet he appears never to have felt the least confusion as to where he belonged. One might begin to explain this by observing that nothing in Longfellow's American background was repressive or narrowing to a man of his temper; that he lacked the cold vanity and intellectuality necessary for any rational style of estrangement; and that his Europe was not ideas, politics, or a possible way of life, but a romantic literary experience. Nevertheless his cultural equilibrium remains a small marvel, and it is reflected in such a poem as "My Lost Youth," where Italian echoes, a classical reference, and a Lapland refrain encountered in German translation are made to blend perfectly with memories of a Maine boyhood.

Longfellow's emotional equilibrium was by no means perfect, and there were periods of intense private depression, anxiety, and hypochondria. One wonders how much these seizures may have proceeded from the unease of self-ignorance, from want of convictions or from that dread of vicissitude which accompanies a love of security. In contrast to Emily Dickinson, say, or Melville, Longfellow had no articulate inwardness, and such a poem as "The Fire of Driftwood" (of which Howard Nemerov has written so well) is atypical in its presentation of a live and nuanced psychology. In religion and morals, Longfellow was neither heretical nor orthodox but conventional, and he embraced a reduced and uncertain Christianity of "the deed, and not the creed" which cannot have been very fortifying against fear or trial. In any case, the poems of Longfellow seem the work of a man who has given all to the exercise of an authentic but limited talent and neglected to grapple with his own heart and mind. The huge work *Christus* is first of all an intellectual failure. "The Saga of King Olaf" is a stunning performance, as Mr. Arvin shows, but the delight in violence which informs it is never brought face to face, in any poem, with the pacifism of that equally fine poem, "The Arsenal at Springfield." Longfellow's last piece of writing, "The Bells of San Blas," is full of felicities, but troubles the reader with a sense not so much of conflict as of discontinuity of attitude. The first ten stanzas express nostalgic regret for the age of faith, but the last stanza (written, Mr. Arvin notes, after a lapse of time) is an abrupt affirmation of progress: "It is daybreak everywhere." Like Tennyson, Longfellow often juxtaposes two quite distinct voices, the one melancholy and desirous of repose, the other positive, edifying, and usually less convincing. "Though he believed in balance," William Charvat has observed, "he did not feel it." And Mr. Arvin makes the right objection to much of Longfellow's moralizing: it is not, as Poe thought, that the didactic has no place in poetry, but that Longfellow's moral lessons are likely to be hand-me-downs rather than trophies of "independent cogitation."

Had Mr. Arvin intended to stir up a Longfellow revival, he might have focused sharply, in his treatment of the work, on those shorter poems which seem most recoverable in view of current taste and reading habits. What he has done is even more interesting—to dismiss very little, and to allot his space with some regard to the pretensions of each work. If this makes for an honorable kind of slow going when ambitious failures are in question, it affords a sense of the whole *oeuvre*, acquaints us with the magnitude of the poet's role as Longfellow saw it and challenges us to appreciate his successes in now disused poetic *genera*. A reviewer cannot comment in detail on commentaries, but Mr. Arvin is to be praised for not misapplying our prevalent criteria—ambiguity and so forth—to Longfellow; what he does is to look for the qualities in Longfellow which, fashionable or not, are worth noting or admiring, and the enquiry is both helpful and aesthetically enlarging. Longfellow emerges as a straightforward poet of mood, sentiment, and story, who was at his best "an accomplished, sometimes an exquisite, craftsman," who dealt in "states of feeling that remain this side of either ecstasy or despair," and whose better work is "worth preserving in some ideal anthology of verse of the second order." Mr. Arvin gives due attention to Longfellow's bold technical experiments in everything from free verse to the eight-stress line, finds "something almost Elizabethan in the range and freshness of Longfellow's work as a translator," and defensibly considers him the best American sonneteer of his century. One agrees, too, that Longfellow's storytelling is well-paced, varied, and thoroughly readable, especially in *Tales of a Wayside Inn,* and that we have to our cost forgotten his talent for humorous narrative. Among many acute passages in Mr. Arvin's critical chapters I particularly prize his observations on the translatableness of Longfellow's "limpid, uneccentric" language, on the poet's "use of literary allusion for purposes of metaphor," and on the associative structure of such poems as "The Jewish Cemetery at Newport."

In an epilogue, Mr. Arvin makes a valuable distinction among three kinds of popular poetry: folk, masscult, and demotic. Folk poetry is preliterate or illiterate; masscult poetry is newspaper verse and the like; demotic poetry is work of genuine literary quality written in response to the emergence of "a very wide body of more or less educated but not sophisticated or exacting readers." That Longfellow consciously responded to such a public may be seen in his praise of "Songs that lowlier hearts feel," in the confident warmth with which he addresses his readers in the "Dedication" to *The Seaside and the Fireside,* and in his letters to G. W. Greene about "The Wreck of the Schooner Hesperus": "I have a great notion of working upon the *people's* feelings. I am going to have it printed on a sheet with a coarse picture on it. I desire a new sensation and a new set of critics. . . ."

Contemporary Russia, with its new literate classes, its scarcity of cheap diversions and its enormous editions of poetry, may be enjoying a kind of officially enforced demotic period; our own "great age of demotic poetry" is past, and Longfellow's reputation went with it. There is much in Longfellow—one has only to think of the powerful *Michael Angelo* or the subtly turned "Snow-Flakes"—which is not popular poetry in any sense, and could easily be more esteemed today. But what of the best of the bulk of his work? Have we no use whatever for the stirring ballad, the clear and modest lyric, the well-told tale? The effect of Mr. Arvin's study is to send us to Longfellow's high-demotic, with an awakened sense of its merits, and to convince us that it would be narrow and improvident to let it go.

For decades prior to my association with the Library of Congress, I had been collecting riddles, translating them, discussing them in my classes, and asking my writing-students to write them. The following lecture was given at the Library in Spring of 1988.

The Persistence of Riddles

LET ME BEGIN with a riddle:

When one doesn't know what it is, then it is something;
but when one knows what it is, then it is nothing.

That is an old Swedish riddle the answer to which is "riddle." And here is another old riddle which says much the same thing:

When first I appear I seem mysterious,
But when I'm explained I am nothing serious.

Some riddles, as you see, take themselves lightly. And I fear that many people nowadays, if they think of the riddle at all, consider it a sort of trick question which, once answered, has no further interest—a silly puzzle which, once clarified, self-destructs, as Rumpelstiltskin did when the miller's daughter spoke his name. Nevertheless, I mean to argue that the riddle or enigma, though playful by nature, is a poetic form of great age, meaning, and persistent vitality.

To ask a riddle is to describe something, darkly and figuratively, without naming it. The description must be true, but it will also involve deliberate difficulty, and the difficulty will lie, for the answerer, in the pondering of suggested analogies and the solution of a seeming paradox. Consider, for example, this great two-line enigma:

> *I tremble at each breath of air,*
> *And yet can heaviest burdens bear.*

Different minds work differently, and to solve a riddle one must be both intuitive and analytic; but let us suppose that we take from that riddle a paradoxical first impression of something very delicate, yet very strong. Then, perhaps, we go fishing in the ocean of analogy for the names of things which a breath of air can stir: feathers, hair, smoke, leaves, a spiderweb, gauze curtains, wood shavings, a sail, a candle's flame. We cast about, too, for bearers of heavy burdens: strong men, freight cars, columns, bridges, pack animals of every kind. As we try to pull these two strands of thought together, we are likely to have mad, tentative visions of tremulous wagons or quaking camels. It may occur to us, then, that a fruit tree, its leaves fluttering and its boughs heavy with apples or pears, could be the answer, and indeed it could. But if we are lucky, we see at last in a flash that the optimum answer is "water," whose surface trembles at each breath of air and which can bear the burden of the heaviest ships.

I think that that water-enigma, in one form or another, has been in this world for a long time. Anthropologists, and historians of the riddle, tell us that the riddle was—as it still is—a major form of oral poetry among all primitive peoples. In early tribal societies, it was playfully used, as often since, in contests of wit, but clearly it was never a trivial puzzle. To make a riddle, or to answer one, was to see the peculiar qualities of an object or creature, to discern its resemblances to other forms and forces, and to have an insight into the relatedness of all phenomena, the reticulum of the world. The riddle was thus an expression of imaginative or spiritual power, and as such was employed in the settling of disputes and the winning of brides, in burial rites, fertility rites, and other religious or magical ceremonies. However we may now conceive of riddles, it is plain that at their inception they had sacred uses, and were a way of approaching the spirits of things.[1]

Surely some of the enigmas of our remote forebears have reached us, little altered, by way of folk tradition; and surely their sense of the riddle's power survives in those folktales whose heroes gain the hand of a princess, or gain their freedom from an ogre, by the asking or solving of enigmas. But let me now move to the ground of recorded history and say a sketchy word or two about the status of the riddle in Western culture. The story was sometimes told, in ancient Greece, that Homer died of embarrassment because of his failure to guess a riddle about body lice. That is an unlikely story, but it indicates the prestige of dark sayings and enigmas among the Greeks. For them, the riddle was an esteemed poetic form; it was written by Pindar, Theocritus, and many another, and there is a wealth of riddles collected in the Palatine Anthology. The most famous of Greek enigmas is the one which the Sphinx posed and Oedipus fathomed:

> *What goes on four legs in the morning light,*
> *On two at noontide, and on three at night?*

Oedipus guessed rightly that the answer to that was "man," since a man goes on all fours as an infant, walks on two feet in the noon of life, and in old age gets around on two legs and a cane. Oedipus's solution of that enigma was of course as ironic, in the light of later events, as those ambiguous and riddling oracles which came out of Delphi; the great puzzle-solver Oedipus could not solve, until it was horribly too late, the puzzle of his own origin. Plato in his *Republic* speaks somewhat patronizingly of riddles, but that dialogue, as we remember, is rather tough on poetry in general. Aristotle's *Poetics,* on the other hand, treats the riddle with respect, defining it as a kind of poetry which presents facts under the guise of "impossible metaphors." Since riddles "consist of metaphors," Aristotle's respect for them may be measured by the high value that he places upon the making of metaphor, which in his opinion is the one poetic ability which cannot be taught or learned. "It is," he says, "the mark of genius, for to make good metaphors implies an intuitive perception of the similarity in dissimilars."

The major event in Latin riddle-making came in the fourth or fifth century, when a man known as Symphosius produced a series of one hundred enigmas in three-line hexameters. Symphosius's riddle-poems were faithful to folk tradition in that they concerned themselves largely with natural things and the common objects of everyday life: snow, hammer, cloud, ship, spider, and so on. At the same time, Symphosius enhanced the riddle by clothing it in finished poetic technique, and in language of much subtlety and grace. Here, in translation, is a specimen of Symphosius's work:

> *Four equal sisters equidistant run*
> *As if they vied in strength and speed, but none*
> *Gains on another, and their task is one.*

The answer to that is *rotae,* wheels. It might be convenient, at this point, to apply Aristotle to Symphosius, and show how a metaphor can be made into a riddle. A metaphor compares two things, but in a selective manner, stressing the ways in which they are alike and excluding the ways in which they are not alike. If I say that a woman's eyes are stars, I mean only that they are bright and heavenly; I don't mean, for example, that they consist of gases. In this riddle of Symphosius, the fundamental metaphor is that the wheels of a cart are runners, since both wheels and runners move swiftly over the ground. Symphosius has, in two steps, turned that metaphor into a riddle. The first step was to allow an element of unlikeness into the metaphor, revising it to read, "Wheels are just like runners, except that they don't compete." The next step was to delete the first term of the comparison—wheels—and to turn the remainder into a question: "We are noncompetitive runners. What's our name?" That is pretty much what Symphosius's riddle says. Because the notion of runners not competing seems "impossible" or absurd, we are challenged to make sense of it somehow. In the process we unearth the original metaphor and the hidden answer, "wheels."

Here now is another of Symphosius's riddles, the answer to which is "river and fish":

> *Sweet purlings in an earth-walled inn resound.*
> *Within that inn, a silent guest is found.*
> *Together, guest and inn are onward bound.*

Symphosius did not know, as we do, that, far from being silent, fish can be quite noisy. Still, it is a beautiful enigma, and as scholars tell us, the enigmas of Symphosius prompted and influenced most of the widespread riddle writing of the Middle Ages, including that of the learned English ecclesiastics Aldhelm and Tatwine, in the seventh and eighth centuries. Out of the same English period, and preserved in the famous Exeter Book, came ninety-odd anonymous riddles in the Anglo-Saxon tongue. Many of these had considerable verve, wit, and beauty, and it is fair to say that, in what survives to us of the earliest English literature, the riddle was an important poetic form. Here, in translation, is a minor sample of Anglo-Saxon riddling:

> *I saw in a corner   something swelling,*
> *Rearing, rising,   and raising its cover.*
> *A lovely lady,   a lord's daughter,*
> *Buried her hands   in that boneless body,*
> *Then covered with a cloth   the puffed-up creature.*

The clean answer to that is "bread," but you are quite right in feeling that this riddle, like many riddles, suggests an additional, off-color answer, as a kind of bonus.

I do not propose to examine in detail the history of riddles in the Renaissance, because I only wish to show, in a cursory way, that the riddle was in the past a valued form of poetry, and that it had its great ages and gifted practitioners. Suffice it to say that, with the advent of printing, there was a lively and continuing demand, all over Europe, for collections of folk or popular enigmas on the one hand, and of literary enigmas on the other; and that any survey of Renaissance riddling would include such august names as Leonardo, Galileo, Cervantes, Rabelais, Wyatt, Shakespeare, and even King James I. What ultimately led to a change in people's conception of the riddle was the gradual divergence between the folk riddle and its literary counterpart. By the latter part of the seventeenth century, the making and guessing of riddles had become a sophisticated amusement in the salons of Paris, and was practiced by such wits as the Abbé Cotin. The enigma also became a regular feature in fashionable magazines, like the double-crostic or cryptogram of our own day. Somewhat later, in England, there was a similar highbrow craze, and the chief figure in this English "riddlemania" was Jonathan Swift.

Swift's riddles are elegant and often delightful. Consider a short portion of his riddle about the corkscrew:

> A *new and wondrous Art I show*
> *Of raising Spirits from below;*
> *In* Scarlet *some, and some in* White,
> *They rise, walk round, yet never fright.*
> *In at each* Mouth *the* Spirits *pass,*
> *Distinctly seen as through a Glass:*
> *O'er* Head *and* Body *make a Rout,*
> *And drive at last all* Secrets *out:*
> *And still, the more I show my Art,*
> *The more they* open every Heart.

That is neatly executed, it is full of good wordplay, and it amusingly echoes St. Paul and the aphorism *in vino veritas*. And yet its voice is not the ancient voice of riddle, with its lingering overtones of religion and magic. What speaks to us, in those riddles which seem to us ancient, is the voice of a common thing or creature somehow empowered to express, in an encoded fashion, the mystery of its being. Or if it is a human voice we hear, there is something shamanistic or oracular about it. In Swift's kind of riddle, by contrast, the voice is that of a clever party guest who is entertaining us with a guessing game. He teases us, and displays the resources of his wit, by giving us couplet after couplet, each containing yet another hint as to the answer. This additive technique makes for long enigmas: the corkscrew riddle is thirty-eight lines long, and Swift's riddle about ink runs on for seven quatrains.

It is not surprising that the riddle turned into a parlor diversion just at the time when Cartesian philosophy and the scientific worldview were conquering men's minds. In an age when the objects and creatures of the physical world were more and more generally conceived of as mere mechanisms, partaking not at all of mind or spirit, and truly describable only by mathematics, how could one take at all seriously a poetic mode in which clouds and clams pretend to speak, or are treated as fellow beings? For Swift and his friends, the riddle was pure fancy, and though they endowed it with ingenuity and polish, they also turned it into light verse. When the eighteenth-century riddle craze petered out, as crazes tend to do, riddles were consigned on the whole to the nursery, there to keep company with charades, conundrums, rebuses, and the like.

In a sense, riddles do belong in the nursery, because all small children are animists who know that cats are persons and that all objects have feelings and personality. Still, it is a comedown for the enigma to consort, in nursery books, with mere verbal games which toy with words, syllables, and letters. You know the sort of thing I mean. "What is the difference between a jeweler and a jailer? *Answer:* A jeweler sells watches but a jailer watches cells." That kind of wordplay is all very well, but it is nothing one would want to hear twice. A riddle, however, is a poem, not a mere verbal trick, and one might wish to hear a good one many times, even if one knows the answer. Take this old folk riddle, for example:

> *As I was walking down the lane,*
> *Out of the dead the living came.*
> *Four there were, and five to be.*
> *Now tell me this riddle or set me free.*

I found that, years ago, in a novel by Conrad Richter, where it appeared as the epigraph to a chapter. It lodged at once in my head, and for weeks I said it to myself at odd moments, enjoying its mixture of the homely and the apocalyptic; but I could not guess its secret. Neither could my friends, although Stanley Kunitz made a fascinating attempt, seeing in those lines the Via Dolorosa, the five wounds of Christ, and the resurrection. In despair, I wrote Mr. Richter, begging for the answer, and he replied that, unfair as it might seem, the answer was "four young birds and an egg in a nest built in a horse's skull."

This answer raises a question. Is fairness an important criterion in judging the merits of an enigma? I think not: a riddle is much more than a puzzle, and we do not evaluate it in terms of sufficiency of evidence or ease of solution. The only thing we ask, as Alice said to the Mad Hatter, is that people not make up riddles which have no answers at all. When first we hear a riddle, we may enjoy it for sound and verbal texture alone, as if it were sheer incantation, a fragment of a lost liturgy, a bit of *poésie pure*; but the experience of a riddle is not complete until the hearer's mind has struggled with it, and an implicit answer has been found or given.

After I had learned the secret of Mr. Richter's folk riddle, I continued to ask it of people, and was astonished, on one occasion, when a Wesleyan student solved it at once. How did he do it? He had been raised on a ranch in Montana, and was no stranger to nests built in animal skulls. Obviously, what you can guess has something to do with what you know. I suppose that I, too, might have solved that enigma out of my own experience, if I had remembered the very similar riddle which Samson asked of the Philistines at his wedding feast:

> *Out of the eater came something to eat,*
> *Out of the strong came something sweet.*

The Philistines did not know that Samson, on one of his journeys to Timnah, had killed a roaring lion with his bare hands; nor did they know that, passing that way again, he had found a swarm of bees in the lion's carcass and eaten of their honey. The Philistines might never have fathomed Samson's riddle, had they not forced Delilah to worm it out of him.

These two enigmas—about birds in a horse's skull, and bees in a lion's carcass—are similar acts of imagination, and they are alike in being very difficult. Both, in fact, are examples of the so-called neck riddle. It was once the custom, in some societies, that a condemned man could save his neck, or a captive gain his liberty, by posing a riddle which his judge or captor could not guess. That is why, I think, the first of these riddles ends with the challenging line, "Now tell me this riddle or set me free." Samson's enigma could be classified, of course, as a wedding riddle; but it is also a neck riddle, because it is outrageously hard, and based on peculiar knowledge, and is posed by a man who, though not a prisoner, was in the midst of his enemies.[2]

I turn now to a few more guessable riddles, beginning with a splendid one which was first called to my attention by David McCord. This riddle is very old; a Latin version of it was copied down in a tenth-century manuscript. It has a double answer: that is to say, it describes two things.

> *White bird featherless*
> *Flew from Paradise,*
> *Pitched on the castle wall;*
> *Along came Lord Landless,*
> *Took it up handless,*
> *And rode away horseless to the King's white hall.*

In all of the riddles I have quoted, there has been some element of paradox or self-contradiction. In this one we encounter a storm of paradoxes—a featherless bird, a lord who has no land, a handless lifter, a horseless rider—and the initial effect is thoroughly confusing. Ultimately we solve the riddle, either by an intuitive pounce or by such plodding thoughts as these: "That white bird can't *be* a bird, because a bird has feathers. What we have, perhaps, is something white that's *like* a bird. How could it be like a bird? It could be like a bird if it *flew*. If this white thing flew from Paradise, would it come from Eden, or from heaven? Ah, now I see: *snow* is the white thing which flies down from the sky, and pitches or settles on the castle wall. And what takes it up must be the sun, that lord of the air who has no earthly domain, who rides across the sky without a horse, who melts the snow and lifts it up—handless—into God's white-clouded heaven."

Like many riddles, this one is strongly pictorial in character, and it gives fascinating proof of the promptness with which we produce mental images, and the stubbornness with which we cling to them. If someone says to me, *think of a white bird,* a white bird appears in my mind's eye; if I am then told to forget about the bird, I find that its image will not go away. Furthermore, if someone says to me, *do not think of a horse,* I think at once of a horse. In the riddle which we have just discussed, there are certain subverted or negated ideas which insist upon composing themselves into a picture—the picture of a noble horseman with a white bird in his hand. Part of our difficulty in solving the riddle is that we must struggle to decompose the vivid picture which we have insisted on making, and see through it to the answer. And even when we have the answer and are enjoying a freshened sense of snow and sun, the horseman and his bird may persist as an afterimage.

The most stunning riddles tend to have a plain darkness of language, such as we find in Shakespeare's phrase "A deed without a name." And they tend to be composed in a rhyming, metrical form which recalls their beginnings in ritual. When, however, the medium is prose, the language (though simple) is generally stylized and rhythmically heightened. Take, for example, this fine prose riddle, full of contradictions, whose hidden subject is not a common thing or creature but a bit of common lore:

> A messenger that could not speak, bearing a letter that was not written, came to a city that had no foundations.

The answer to that is the dove, the olive leaf, and the ark. The likening of Noah's ark to a city may seem strange at first, but it grows on you. The ark, at the time when Noah released his dove, was a kind of hill town, not built upon Ararat but precariously stranded there, and crowded within it was the whole population of the earth.

Here now is a charming enigma which many will recall from childhood:

> *In marble walls as white as milk,*
> *Lined with a skin as soft as silk,*
> *Within a fountain crystal-clear,*
> *A golden apple doth appear.*
> *No doors there are to this stronghold,*
> *Yet thieves break in and steal the gold.*

That rich and curious structure, that doorless stronghold, sounds as if it belonged in a fairy tale or chivalric romance. To someone unused to the aesthetic of riddles, it might seem anticlimactic, after all that marble, silk, and gold, that the answer should be merely "an egg." But that is not how enigmas are to be taken; whatever else they do, they are out to restore for a moment the wonder of ordinary things—to make us amazed, in this case, that an egg should be what it is. Walt Whitman was speaking in the key of this riddle when he said, "a mouse is a miracle sufficient to stagger sextillions of infidels."

One authority defines the riddle as "essentially a metaphor which draws attention to likenesses between unrelated objects." We have had a simple example of that in Symphosius's comparison of wheels to human runners. Here is a little folk riddle which does even more violence to our normal sense of relations:

> Lives in winter,
> Dies in summer,
> And grows with its root upwards.

What we have there is a comparison of an icicle to a plant— an odd sort of plant which does everything in reverse. Most of us, I think, would regard icicles and plants as not belonging to the same context or class of beings; merely to join them with an *and*—merely to say "plants and icicles"—sounds like Lewis Carroll's nonsense talk about "cabbages and kings." Therefore when a riddler, using the bold weapon of metaphor, forces us to contemplate an icicle *as* a plant, it is an imaginative coup; briefly, and in a small way, our sense of the structure of reality is shaken.

If that riddle shakes us a little, the effect of the next one should be seismic.

> Head like a snake,
> Neck like a drake,
> Side like a bream,
> Back like a beam,

> *Tail like a rat,*
> *Foot like a cat.*

At some stage of one's pondering of an enigma, one is likely, as we have seen, to have wild composite ideas, chimerical visions. In this case, one's very first impression is of an incredible monster, a sort of super-sphinx. However, if the mind's eye is particularly agile, it may soon commence to see the poem for what it is: a deconstruction of a greyhound. Much as the egg riddle figuratively described its subject part by part—shell, membrane, white, and yolk—this riddle inventories the parts of a dog in a series of similes; but whereas the egg riddle composed its metaphors into an architectural picture, the greyhound riddle initially consists of violently divergent images. I can tell you, as the owner of a greyhound, that the similes of this riddle are very accurate. The riddle does what almost all good riddles do—it results in a fresh and astonished perception of a creature. And it does something else that riddles do—it explodes for a moment our habitual classifications of phenomena. Just as we were asked to see an icicle as a plant, we are now asked to see a dog as partaking of the qualities of a wooden beam, a reptile, a rodent, a fish, a bird, and a feline. Such confounding of our categories may be seen as a part of the riddle's strategy of deception, but it is also part of the riddle's message. Not only does a riddle offer us, once we have solved it, a yoking of supposedly unrelated things; it also obliges us, in the process of solution, to strike out across the conceptual grid which our minds have imposed upon the world. If an enigma seems to turn upon the word *head*, for example, we find ourselves ransacking the environment for things and creatures to which it might apply: a man, a river, a pin, a bed, a glass of beer, a boil, a parade, a daisy. If we are looking for something which "trembles at each breath of air," our mental safari, as we have seen, will be giddier still. Riddles open a door, as Craig Williamson has said in *A Feast of Creatures,* upon a fluent and "metamorphic" view of the world, in which no comparisons are farfetched and no things are unrelated; they unlimber the mind, making us aware of the arbitrariness of our taxonomy; they restore us briefly to clear-eyed ignorance and a sense of mystery.

It may now seem that I am taking a nursery pastime too seriously, and making excessive claims for what confusing little poems can do to our consciousness. This is only because we are no longer primitive tribesmen, for whom riddles are a cultural instrument of great value and usefulness. Let me return, for a moment, to discussing what I have gathered about the functions of riddle in tribal societies. It seems evident, as Michael Alexander argues in *The Earliest English Poems,* that the religious use of riddles is to serve as imaginative exercises and cryptic formulae with which to draw near the beings and forces of a "noumenous natural world." If riddles also have a magical function, it might be, as some maintain, that the successful solving of riddles at tribal weddings or at planting time insures, by sympathetic magic, the success of the marriage or the corn crop. I have mentioned already the role of enigmas in contests of wit and in the settling of disputes. It is certain also that they have had a mnemonic use in the education of the young, a use which in one past instance survived the transition to literacy: the earliest recorded riddles were found on the tablets of Babylonian schoolchildren. A final function of the riddle, which does not exclude these others, is that it operates in tribal cultures as a kind of Dionysian force. The myths of a tribe, as E. K. Maranda observes, reinforce "the established order" and accepted patterns of thought; its riddle-poetry, however, is subversive of accepted thought patterns, and (as Maranda says) "makes a point of playing with conceptual borderlines, and crossing them, for the pleasure of showing that things are not quite as stable as they appear." This relationship of myth and riddle reflects the need of any society to have, on the one hand, an orderly view of things and, on the other hand, to be capable of mental adjustment and adaptive change. One value of riddles in tribal life, then, is that they give practice in the enlargement and reshuffling of reality.

If we look for familiar analogies to this ancient function of the riddle, we think perhaps of the juxtapositions of surrealist art, which aim to liberate the unconscious; or we think of the Zen koan, a kind of dialogic utterance which induces insight by short-circuiting the everyday mind. The riddle has no such clear assignment nowadays, and is often brushed off as trivial and subliterary. Nevertheless it persists, because its genius is so close to the genius of lyric poetry itself. I shall partially illustrate this point by quoting a little poem by Robert Francis. Francis is writing about a baseball pitcher, but he is also clearly writing about the poet.

PITCHER

His art is eccentricity, his aim
How not to hit the mark he seems to aim at,

His passion to avoid the obvious,
His technique how to vary the avoidance.

The others throw to be comprehended. He
Throws to be a moment misunderstood.

Yet not too much. Not errant, arrant, wild,
But every seeming aberration willed.

Not to, yet still, still to communicate
Making the batter understand too late.

If we see that pitcher as a poet, and the batter as his reader, Francis is talking about how poetry avoids the expected thing, gives the reader pause by such means as obliquity, suggestion, or startling metaphor, and causes him to perform continual double takes. Aristotle speaks in his *Rhetoric* of this pattern of surprise, delay, and excited recognition, observing that metaphor enlivens language by deceiving our expectations. The reader, he says, "who expected something quite different, is all the more aware, from the contrast, that he has learned something. His mind seems to say, 'True enough!—and I never thought of it!'" Aristotle adds, "Good riddles delight us for the same reason; their form is metaphorical, and their solution is an act of learning." If poetry deals in surprise and delayed apprehensions, then the riddle exaggerates an essential characteristic of poetry. If metaphor, the perception of resemblances, is central to poetry, then the riddle operates near that center. If lyric poetry perceives wonder and mystery, so does the riddle. And if poetry may be seen as offering a continuing critique of our sense of order, the riddle has its peculiar aptitude for that.

Thus, though they have long been slighted by common opinion, riddles are irrepressible; they so belong to poetry's nature that if we scan American verse of the last two centuries, riddle and the spirit of riddle crop up surprisingly often. There are enigmas, for instance, among the juvenilia of William Cullen Bryant. Longfellow translated from the Anglo-Saxon a poem about the grave which speaks the true tongue of enigma in such lines as "For thee was a house built/ Ere thou wast born. . . . Doorless is that house,/ And dark it is within." Emerson's conception of a transcendent One, in which all distinctions and contraries are dissolved, produced the riddling paradoxes of his poem "Brahma." And in Emerson's "Uriel," we may hear the deepest drift of riddle in those cryptic verses which sweep aside all categories, all drawing of lines between this and that:

> *Line in nature is not found;*
> *Unit and universe are round;*
> *In vain produced, all rays return;*
> *Evil will bless, and ice will burn.*

Of American writers, it is Poe who most challenges the reader not only to read him but also to solve him; one of his definitions of poetry—as the art of making "novel combinations"—could be a good short definition of riddle-making as well. One of Poe's most familiar poems, "The Haunted Palace," is best described as an elaborate enigma not unlike the egg riddle which I lately quoted: part by part, it describes a man's head, with its hair, eyes, teeth, and lips, as palace architecture, and the man's loss of reason as the overthrow of a king within. The famous catalogues of Walt Whitman's "Song of Myself," with their headlong jumbling of disparate images, are akin to riddles in their bracketing of things supposedly unrelated and their vision of a metamorphic world in which all things are of one nature. To be sure, Whitman's catalogues work less by metaphor than by juxtaposition, parallel grammar, and manic impetus; still, we are not surprised when, in the midst of one of his inventories of everything, he modulates into riddle and speaks not of the moon but of "the crescent child that carries its own full mother in its belly."

Emily Dickinson wrote so many riddles that Dolores Dyer Lucas has devoted an entire critical book to them; Dickinson's great popularity is one reason why the riddle may seem to some of us a living modern form. We all know the exquisite hummingbird riddle which begins "A route of Evanescence/ With a revolving Wheel," and there are others—about frost, or a snake, or a railroad train—which are frequently met in anthologies. This is one of her best:

> *Some things that fly there be—*
> *Birds—Hours—the Bumblebee—*
> *Of these no Elegy.*
>
> *Some things that stay there be—*
> *Grief—Hills—Eternity—*
> *Nor this behooveth me.*
>
> *There are that, resting, rise.*
> *Can I expound the skies?*
> *How still the Riddle lies!*

In this poem Emily Dickinson feels that she is called upon—that it behooves her—to write an elegy. Her subject is not a thing that flies, nor is it a thing that stays; rather, it is something, as we learn in line seven, that flies and stays at once, that both rests and rises. What that could be, we have been prepared to guess by such words as "Grief" and "Eternity," and by the fact that an elegy is often a poem of mourning and comfort, occasioned by a death. Where are we, then? As so often in Dickinson, we are in a bed-chamber where someone has just died—whose soul presumably has risen, and whose body remains below.

One of Dolores Lucas's best observations is that in most of

Dickinson's riddles the answers are simple, while the real complexity of the poems lies in their expressed ambiguity of attitude. That is the case here. All of the poem's talk about flying and staying, resting and rising, conventionally assumes that the soul survives the body and may go to heaven; yet at the close of the poem, confronted by the riddle of a corpse, Dickinson cannot "expound" that elegiac consolation. The poem ends in doubt, or in speechlessness.

Robert Frost once wrote the following little enigma:

> *He has dust in his eye and a fan for a wing,*
> *A leg akimbo with which he can sing,*
> *And a mouthful of dye-stuff instead of a sting.*

That a grasshopper has a singing leg is no more than the truth, but in the setting of a riddle we see it for the marvel that it is. Frost called that tercet "One Guess" in his *Collected Poems*; at an earlier time it bore the title "My What-Is-It." Are there other riddles, other what-is-its, in Frost's work? Strictly speaking, no; but when the ancestral voice of riddle surfaces in Frost's poems, as it does, it is generally a sign that no easy message or solution should be looked for. As with the Dickinson poem I quoted, riddling makes way for the expression of ambivalence. The enigmatic line, "Something there is that doesn't love a wall," may seem to promise an unqualified judgment as to walls and what they mean, but the rest of the poem, if I may say so, is very much on the fence. Frost's most oracularly riddling lines are surely these:

> *There is a house that is no more a house*
> *Upon a farm that is no more a farm*
> *And in a town that is no more a town*

—and those lines are from "Directive," a poem so fiercely ironic, so divided against itself, that, as Randall Jarrell said, it is both consoling and heartbreaking at once.

If I had the time and wit, I would explore the presence of riddle-like strategies in certain lyrics of recent decades—asking, for instance, what happens to the reader's mind when a poem defers the statement of its literal subject for six or a dozen lines. I would consider Elizabeth Bishop's poem "The Monument" as an enigma, and discuss how W. H. Auden, in the second section of his "Anthem for St. Cecilia's Day," has music itself speak to us, conveying its otherness in the mode of riddle. But I will return to riddles proper and conclude by offering a few proofs that the muse of riddle has lately been with us.

Some years ago, Howard Nemerov wrote to me as follows:

> This winter past, on a Greyhound bus in a snowstorm, it came to me to write five riddles in verse; whence arose a probably impossible ideal for poetry, thus:
>
> 1. a poem must seem very mysterious.
>
> 2. but it must have an answer (= a meaning) which is precise, literal, and total; that is, which accounts for every item in the poem.
>
> 3. it must remain very mysterious, or even become more so, when you know the answer.

It is fascinating, I think, that a contemporary poet should recapitulate history by deriving from the riddle an ideal for the lyric. Here is one of the riddles which came to Nemerov in that Greyhound bus:

> *I am the combination to a door*
> *Which fools and wise with equal ease undo.*

Your unthought thoughts are changes still unread
In me, without whom nothing's to be said.

The answer to that is "the alphabet." May Swenson has written many riddles, and many poems which partake of riddle. This one is called "Living Tenderly":

My body a rounded stone
with a pattern of smooth seams.
My head a short snake,
retractive, projective.
My legs come out of their sleeves
or shrink within,
and so does my chin.
My eyelids are quick clamps.
My back is my roof.
I am always at home.
I travel where my house walks.
It is a smooth stone.
It floats within the lake,
or rests in the dust.
My flesh lives tenderly
inside its bone.

That, of course, is a turtle. And now, in an exquisite little poem by Donald Justice, a thing—a common object—is speaking to us:

Mine to give, mine to offer
No resistance. Mine
To receive you, mine to keep
The shape of our nights.

That was a pillow speaking. Finally, I want to quote from
J. R. R. Tolkien, whose book *The Hobbit* was not long ago a sort
of sacred text for the young. You may recall that in the fifth
chapter, there is a riddle contest between Bilbo Baggins and a
slimy creature named Gollum, and that Bilbo saves his life by
asking a species of neck riddle. Here is one of Tolkien's riddles:

> *Alive without breath,*
> *As cold as death;*
> *Never thirsty, ever drinking,*
> *All in mail never clinking.*

If that beautiful fish enigma is still in the heads of those who
were young in the sixties, perhaps we can say that the riddle is
still alive and well, not only as an elementary presence in lyric,
but in and as itself.

NOTES

This essay is the work of an amateur, but of an amateur who has dipped, to his profit, into a small portion of the existing scholarship on riddles. I have drawn information or material from the following scholar-collectors not mentioned in my text: Mark Bryant, Archer Taylor, Iona and Peter Opie, and Lillian Morrison. And I am also indebted to Raymond Ohl, Tony Augarde, William Blakemore, Ian Hamnet, and Andrew Welsh. My authorities are not responsible for the fact that, in this breezy piece, I have streamlined the history of the riddle form and treated all primitive societies as essentially one.

1. That the primitive riddle was more religious than magical may be seen if we compare the riddle with that other early and universal form of poetry, the charm. The normal language of the charm is esoteric in character, it being understood (as George T. Flom tells us of Anglo-Saxon charm literature) that if the everyday name of a thing were employed, the charm could not magically control it. Riddle and charm are thus alike in that each contains a hidden name; clearly, however, the two forms had different roles in the imaginative economy of our forebears, the charm being an incantatory instrument of coercion and the riddle being chiefly concerned, as Andrew Welsh says, with "vision and knowledge."

2. In connection with "As I was walking down the lane," the reader may be interested in some evidence of the wanderings and mutations of that riddle. The poet Daniel Mark Epstein lately sent me this version, which is ascribed by local tradition to a slave in Dorchester County, on Maryland's Eastern Shore.

DORCHESTER SLAVE'S RIDDLE

I came out and in again,
living from the dead came,
there are six, seven there will be;
answer this riddle or set me free.

And I find that in his book *High Island* (Harper & Row, 1974), the Irish poet Richard Murphy has incorporated a variant of the riddle in the following poem, which is itself a variation on the neck riddle:

GALLOWS RIDDLE

Hangman: *In I went, out again,*
Death I saw, life within,
Three confined there, one let free:
Riddle me that or hung you'll be.

Tinker: *Five maggoty sheep I stole*
Tangled me on the gallows tree,
Now my tongue must riddle me free:
A nest of birds in an old man's skull.

This memorial tribute was read at a meeting of the National Institute of Arts and Letters in 1990.

May Swenson

MAY SWENSON was not much given to self-absorption or self-portraiture, but in one of her later poems we find her looking at herself and seeing the lineaments of her mother and father. "I look at my hand," she says—

> *I look at my hand and see*
> *it is also his and hers;*
> *the pads of the fingers his,*
>
> > *the wrists and knuckles hers.*
> > *In the mirror my pugnacious eye*
> > *and ear of an elf, his;*
> >
> > > *my tamer mouth and slant*
> > > *cheekbones hers.*

That gives us a glimpse of May Swenson, though I should like to qualify it; she did indeed inherit a brow and set of eye which were capable of pugnacity, but what I mostly saw in her blue eyes was forthrightness, independence, good nature, and a great power of attention. She had an appealing and sociable Swedish face, with fair hair cut in a Dutch bob across the forehead.

May's parents came over from Sweden and settled in Logan, Utah, were converted to Mormonism, and had ten children of whom she was the eldest. After her graduation from the college where her father taught mechanical engineering, and after a spell of journalism in Utah, she came east and lived, for most of her writing life, in the New York area. Nevertheless, she remained Western in many ways. She had a great relish for wild nature and a knowing sympathy with wild creatures; her poems are full of tents and cabins and the out-of-doors; when an Amy Lowell Poetry Travelling Scholarship took her to Europe for the first time, at the age of forty-one, she and a companion "bought a small French car and tenting equipment" and, in their travels through France, Spain, and Italy, spent most of their nights under canvas. Effete Easterners do not make the grand tour in that fashion. The poems are Western, too, in their openness of tone and diction; even at their trickiest, they are made out of plain American words. The breezy spontaneity of their technique—the lineation and spacing, the playful random rhyming—makes sometimes for a lack of finish, but more usually seems in perfect accord with the swift vigor of her spirit.

One thing she did not bring east was Mormonism, or any other kind of church religion. This did not result in any sense of loss or any want of scope. What May put in the place of any supernatural view was a truly knowledgeable awareness, rare among poets of our time, of the world as perceived and probed by contemporary science. An initial reaction to the mention of science, in connection with May's poetry, might be to think of her famous descriptive power, her ability to make us see objects sharply and in new ways. It was this talent that led Robert Lowell to say, "Miss Swenson's quick-eyed poems should be hung with permanent fresh-paint signs." When we talk about Marianne Moore or Elizabeth Bishop, we soon find ourselves quoting their brilliant captures and sightings of things, and so it is with May Swenson, who admired them both; one thinks of how, in a poem of May's, young skunk cabbages rise up out of a swamp like "Thumbs of old/ gloves, the nails/ poked through// and curled." Or one remembers the lines in which she conveys the shape, motion, and wake of an East River tugboat: "A large shoe/ shuffles the floor of water,/ leaving a bright scrape."

But this power to observe things keenly is not all that May Swenson shares with the scientist, as may be learned from an essay which she wrote for the Voice of America in the sixties, and entitled "The Experience of Poetry in a Scientific Age." What is central in that essay is its acceptance, as a model for poetry, of our cognitive situation as described by the atomic physicist, for whom the swarming particles that constitute the cosmos are not knowable in themselves, but are inevitably altered by our instruments of perception. If that is the way we know the universe, then the unit of reality is not an objective recording of data, or an imposition of order, but an occasion of interplay or dialogue between perceiver and world—what Whitehead called a "prehension." May's poetry is full of such moments of interplay—perceptual games and experiments in seeing that are grounded in a serious theory of knowledge. Her little poem "Forest," for example, begins this way:

> *The pines, aggressive as erect tails of cats,*
> *bob their tips when the wind freshens.*

It then proceeds to depict the pine forest entirely in the key of cat—discovering a feline character in its brindled colors, its humped and springy floor, its lashed and winking boughs, and the purring sound of the wind going through them. This might seem merely a fanciful imposition, a virtuoso feat, were it not for the fact that the poet's accurate metaphors realize the forest more vividly than any botanist's language could do—so that the poet in her turn is acted upon, and the revealed strangeness of the scene creates in her a mood of forest-fear, of panic. The poem thus ends with these lines:

My neck-hairs rise. The feline forest grins

behind me. Is it about to follow?
Which way out through all these whiskered yawns?

At the beginning of the essay to which I referred, May Swenson says this about the poetic experience: "I see it based in a craving to get through the curtains of things as they *appear*, to things as they *are*, and then into the larger, wilder space of things as they are *becoming*." That sentence contains the whole drama of May Swenson's poetry, the passion that underlies her playfulness. Though she knows that the senses can deceive us, it is through the alert, surprising use of those instruments that she seeks to break through to reality, refusing (as she says) "to take given designations for granted" or "to accept without a second look the name or category of a thing for the thing itself." Her poetry is, in fact, at war with names and designations, insofar as they can occlude our vision or foreclose our curiosity. *God*, she tells us in one of her poems, is a name that men have given to the idea of changelessness, and such a name is delusive in a world where everything moves and alters, where all is "breathing change." As for lesser names—such as *stream*, *flower*, or *roller coaster*—it is a special and frequent strategy of hers to withhold them, so that the poem may look more closely, naively, and inquiringly at the things to which they refer.

The riddle is an ancient poetic form in which an object is darkly described and its name withheld. May wrote a good many fine riddles about such objects as *egg* and *fire* and *butterfly*—enough so that a selection could be made "for young readers" and published in 1966 under the title of *Poems to Solve*. We are foolishly inclined nowadays to look at such poems as kid stuff, but to see May Swenson's riddles as part of her whole poetic

enterprise is to rediscover the dignity of the form. Richard How-
ard was right to say that, in this aspect of her work, May wrote
"a poetry that goes back to Orpheus." A riddle is at first a con-
cealment, the withholding of a name; but as and when we solve
its dark metaphor, the riddle is a revelation, giving us not only
a name, but an object freed from clichés of perception and seen
with wonder as if for the first time. Most of May's poems, of
course, are not riddles, yet again and again they make use of
riddling strategy to produce their revelations and to enforce an
intense participation by the reader. In a poem called "Mother-
hood," we seem at first to be looking at an unusually ugly naked
woman, who is holding a skinny, louse-ridden child to her
breast; yet by the end of the poem, when the mother is proudly
swinging from bar to bar with the infant clinging to her armpit
hair, we have somehow been led to see her as beautiful. One
reason for the success of the piece is that nowhere in title or
text are we given such words as *ape* or *zoo* or *cage*—words that
would allow us to relax into preconceptions. The poem is by no
means obscure; one begins rather early to know the "answer";
and yet this withholding of a few clinching words prompts one
to look hard at the object, be limber in one's response to it, and
rejoice at last in another creature's splendid life.

That is what May meant by *getting through*, a process in
which the poet transforms the object by some imaginative ap-
proach, draws closer to it by repeated acts of attention, and is
at last, herself, transformed by the object. We have this pattern
at its simplest in a poem called "While Seated on a Plane."
There, the poet looks out of a window and sees the cloudscape
as a great parlor full of soft chairs and couches. She dreams of
walking out to make herself comfortable in that "celestial fur-
niture," but is perplexed by its vast, turbulent changes of form.

She solves the problem through a further act of imagination, in which she forsakes her own shape and substance and conceives herself as perpetually "deformed/ and reformed." "One must be a cloud," as the poem says, "to occupy a house of cloud." Playful and charming as the poem is, it is like many another poem of May's in its passionate wish to cancel the distinction between subject and object and to be at one with the portion of reality described. That is the impulse behind the "shaped poems," of which she wrote so many, and of which my favorite is a study of wave behavior called "How Everything Happens." These creations, which dispose their words on the page to suggest the form or motion of the subject, represent not only pictorial wit but the desire of the poem to become what it is about.

Like Emily Dickinson, who much influenced her, May lived in the universe. No poet of our day has said and conjectured so much about stars and space. But whereas Dickinson's soul could expand to the limits of space and beyond, May's universe is ultimately that of the astronomer and physicist—a storm of galaxies and particles still uncharted by the mind, in which the mind itself may seem anomalous and lonely. Such a reality can be frightening, and May's poems have their moments of Pascalian dread; but her prevalent mood is one of delight. That needs no explaining, I think; when art is morose, we want to know why, but joy requires no reasons. It is clear, however, that she trusted her craving to get beyond the self and her rapture in making imaginative fusions with the other. In consequence, her poems find the erotic in all forms of natural energy and, whether they speak of nebulae or horses or human love, are full of a wonderfully straightforward and ebullient sexuality. As for death, she approaches it often in a spirit of Whitmanian merging. Here are the opening lines of a sprightly late poem called "Ending":

> *Maybe there is a Me inside of me*
> *and, when I lie dying, he*
> *will crawl out. Through my toe.*
> *Green on the green rug, and then*
> *white on the wall, and then*
> *over the windowsill, up the trunk*
> *of the apple tree, he*
> *will turn brown and rough and warty*
> *to match the bark. . . .*

She is poking fun at conventional notions of the soul, but there is no missing the fact that blessedness, for her, would be a state of perfect transparency. I do not know where May is now, but her poems continue to mix with time, and to be part of the vitality of the world.

John Ciardi

JOHN CIARDI was one of the first real poets I ever met. After World War II, in which he had served as an aerial gunner, he went to Harvard to be a Briggs-Copeland instructor in English. I turned up there in the same year of 1946, to be at first a graduate student, and, later, John's colleague in the English faculty. John was thirty when we met, five years older than I, and was already a well-known and much-published poet. But he didn't lord it over me, and we were friends at once, beginning a never-finished conversation about words and poetry, and a forty-year anagrams competition, the last bouts of which took place this year in our adjoining Key West houses.

Cambridge, in the latter forties and early fifties, was experiencing what literary historians would call a poetic ferment. There were many poets about, too many to name, and they gathered in small evening groups to read their poems aloud and fish for praise. There was much excitement about poetic drama, and verse-plays old and new were presented in lofts and parish houses and on college stages. The poetry reading, a form of concert which had once given pleasure only if the poet were of Robert Frost's magnitude, suddenly became so popular that anyone who had published a book, or a few poems in *Accent* or the *Atlantic*, could draw a crowd. And these new crowds wanted not only to hear poetry but also to hear *about* it in endless symposia. John Ciardi was a part of all this, as was I; and for several summers, furthermore, we lectured about poetry on alternate days at the Bread Loaf Writers' Conference in Vermont. John's difference from the rest of us was that from any lectern, or on any stage, he spoke in a fine strong voice, challenging and amusing his hearers, never referring to notes, thinking on his feet, drawing on his exceptional memory for quotations and instances. He was, from the first, a natural performer.

John was esteemed at Harvard, and had his close associations there, but it was never his ambition to blend into the Yard or the Square. He lived his own life over in Medford, where he wrote poems for half or all of every night. One evening, when John and Judith asked us to Medford for dinner, my wife and I found large photographs of the poet, ruggedly handsome in a dignified suit and tie, propped everywhere on chair seat, couch, and tabletop. These were publicity pictures, and we were to help choose the best one. We learned with astonishment that John had an agent, as nobody else did, that he was going on the road, and that he meant to talk not merely in college auditoriums but in community lecture halls and the clubrooms of Hokinson-land, vying there with Cornelia Otis Skinner and John Mason Brown. So he proceeded to do. His wish to address a large, general public was reflected also in his famous 1950 anthology, *Mid-Century American Poets,* which presented fifteen writers roughly of his own generation, among them Theodore Roethke, Elizabeth Bishop, Robert Lowell and Randall Jarrell. John's introduction to the anthology differed from the usual thing in that it was not aimed at highbrows; it was recruiting literature, aimed at intelligent lay persons who needed to be taught how to read poems, how to despise uplift and sentimentality, how to constitute an audience for a new American poetry which, John felt, had at last outgrown the English influence and could treat of realities in a charged version of our native speech. John's apostolic urge, his urge to "bring the audience to the poem," took him beyond the academy onto the road, into radio and television, into poetry publishing, and into many years of reviewing, editing, and column-writing for the *Saturday Review*. He became, in his own self-mocking words, "the well-known poet, critic, editor, and middle-high/ aesthete of the circuit." I think that, without ever lowering his standards for poetry, he enlivened many minds and accomplished something of his mission. The main negative result of his leaving the academy for wider arenas was, I suspect, the relative neglect of his poetry by academic critics.

Rereading John Ciardi's work, especially if one approaches him through the *Selected Poems* published two years ago, one is struck by its profoundly autobiographical nature. I don't mean that he was a "confessional" poet; he was too full of modesty and humor to be the histrionic central figure in his own work. But he knew always that his view of things was inseparable from the special conditions of his life. In Part I of the *Selected*, the poems all have to do with his childhood and youth as the son of southern-Italian immigrants in Boston's North End and later in Medford. His memories of that uprooted Italian world are full of love and gusto, but also of exasperation and hurt. When John was only three, his father's death left him feeling disinherited; and a larger disinheritance was his inability, as a bright first-generation American child, to find sustenance in his tribal ethos—in Mediterranean peasant traditions or a Catholicism which seemed to him superstitious and oppressive. He said in his *Lives of X* that he had been born in the Middle Ages, adding, "Sometimes I think I've made it out of the dark/ but not into the light."

Some things he did inherit: a feeling for the earth, for natural things, for physical work, for the rituals of eating and drinking, for family affection and solidarity. In Part II of the *Selected*,

all the poems have to do with his happy marriage, his house-
hold, and his children. Of those things, and of friendship, he
was sure, if so thoroughly skeptical a man may be said to have
been sure of anything. John's raging skepticism had two aspects.
One was an anger at God for being no better than a possibility;
he felt cheated of the repose of certainty, and of the tradition
and ceremony which can sweeten life. In one poem he says of
himself and his young family,

> I wish we were Jews and could say
> The names of what made us.
> I could weep by slow waters for my son
> Who has no history, no name
> he knows long, no ritual from which he came,
> and no fathers but the forgotten.

The other side of John's skepticism was a rigorous mistrust
of all pretensions to know what we don't know; all cocksure
theories of divinity or nature; all ideologies which invest history
or the state with high purpose; all falsely sanguine views of the
human lot or of human behavior. One of his poems ends by
saying, "Not everything that happens/ Is a learning experience.
Maybe nothing is." And the man who had flown so many bomb-
ing missions over Japan could write, "High reasons and low
causes make a war." I could offer fifty other quotations illus-
trating John's sense of the limits of knowledge and the limita-
tions of mankind. Only once did I ever hear him overestimate
human beings. That was back in the days when instant shaving
lather was first being marketed in cans. "People won't buy the
stuff," he told me. "My godfather John Follo was a barber, and
I know that the only decent lather is worked up on the face."
He was right about lather, but for a moment he had forgotten

about men's laziness and subjection to advertising. As a rule, in poetry or out, John saw eye to eye with La Rochefoucauld, who traced our best and worst motives to self-interest. The notion, for instance, of altruism—of a wholly selfless benevolence—set John's teeth on edge; he believed in goodness, but not that unearthly kind.

The insistence of John Ciardi's skepticism has led some readers to find him too negative. The poems are indeed insistent; John could not write his best love poem without mentioning again, in passing, the unlikelihood of heaven and the certainty of death. But the poems are in fact very positive: they are the utterance of a man who wishes to embrace the world with his eyes open, on what seem to him honest terms. Even when he writes of those he loves, John does not fail to mention their follies and defects; but the important thing is that he, as another faulty creature, loves them anyway. And so it is when he speaks of the catalpa in his yard: most of the year, he says, it is a nuisance, its branches breaking in the wind, its pods strewing the lawn; but in late June its white flowers are a miracle, and the miracle is what matters. John was an observant and celebratory poet of natural things; if he, like Robert Frost, could find no spiritual revelations in nature, that did not deprive him of wonder, and he wrote excellently of wild turkeys landing or egrets in flight. Art was another thing he celebrated, the art of others and his own practice of art, of which he wrote that "clean white paper waiting under a pen/ Is the gift beyond history and hurt and heaven."

John's early work was done in resourceful rhyme and in strict meters expressively handled: I think of the toughly witty poem "Elegy Just in Case," with its subverted echoes of Shakespeare, or the poignant and elevated "Sea Burial." At any time, as in the later poem "Minus One," it was in his power to be formally dazzling. But the characteristic Ciardi poem is not a full-dress performance: it is technically muted and relaxed; colloquial; ruminative; it has the movement of developing thought; it pauses to toy with its own words; it gets carried away by memory or example; it ends with an offhand air. Often such poems begin with a trivial occasion and proceed, in the key of comedy, toward what proves after all to be a serious theme. One poem, for instance, begins with the poet lying sweaty and spread-eagled in a bedroom whose air conditioner has failed; his posture reminds him that he lacks the ideal human proportions described by Vitruvius and drawn by Leonardo; and that starts him off on a train of thought which includes Praxiteles, the Platonic ideas, and the notion of man as God's image. Sometimes the mood of such a poem is darker, even to the point of sadness. Like Wallace Stevens, John lived day by day in a dubious universe, but he did not make Stevens's prudent exclusions. His poems, unlike Stevens's, are full of human attachments, and of humane concern, and given his view of life some sadness was inescapable. The late poem "Being Called" is a boldly sad piece about how hard it is for aging men to admit that they are not what once they were; at the end of it we have a glimpse of John himself in his Key West patio:

> ... *I am in Florida,*
> *a February rose nodding*
>
> *over my toast and coffee in a soft*
> *expensive breeze I can afford,*
> *in a sun I buy daily, gladly,*
> *on a patio under a lime tree.*
> *There is a pleasantness. With luck*

it is a kindly long trip down
from cramming winter to this basking
knowledge of nothing. And from Miami
on the make-do transistor, a cracked
wrong quaver that began as Mozart.

Those lines are rueful, to say the least, in their portrayal of declining powers. What balances the ruefulness, of course, is the good metaphor of the southward journey and that brilliant image of the quavering transistor. The fact is that John wrote well to the end.

Last winter I walked into John's living room and said, "I've just noticed that the words *must* and *stum,* which are anagrams of each other, can both mean 'unfermented grape juice.'" Some people, perhaps, would not be stirred by such an announcement. John, however, rose and said, "You don't say! Let's look up the etymologies." Out of his lifelong obsession with words, he wrote many of his best magazine columns; in recent years, his PBS radio broadcasts on word origins were relished by a nationwide audience; his *Browser's Dictionary,* of which a final volume is yet to come, is full of intriguing and opinionated researches into the transformations of language. If John was always one of the prolific poets of his generation, he was also a very diversified industry; I must add to the enterprises already mentioned that he wrote a cracking good textbook called *How Does a Poem Mean?,* and that his much-honored volumes of children's verse were the sort of verse that children actually like to read. Finally, there is the celebrated undertaking which the *Times* obituary rightly mentions in its first sentence: his rendering of Dante's *Commedia.* John's translation simplified the rhyme-structure of the poem, for the sake of greater fidelities, and it is the glory of his version that it matches Dante's whole range of voices, being beautifully harsh where Dante is harsh and, what is most difficult of all, simple where Dante is simple. I think there is no doubt that John Ciardi gave the English language its best *Commedia*. As I said on another occasion, if it were human to be satisfied, John might have been well satisfied.

He had certain faults, as his own honesty forces me to admit: he could raise his voice, and throw his weight around, and be difficult. But he had many good qualities. He was a courageous man, and a truth-teller. He was also that rare thing, a poet with a finite view of his own merits. He was a warmhearted man, a lively companion, and a loyal friend. Addio, Giovanni.

Glimpses

I

*Many years ago, I was asked to write something for a
projected (but never published) collection of reminiscences
of Dylan Thomas.*

JOHN BRINNIN'S BOOK performed an essential service in in-
forming the many who mistook Dylan for Priapus, or Punchi-
nello, or the Life Force—a living rebuke to all stuffy people—
that he was an ill man blundering toward his own death. He
and I stood once in front of someone's fireplace trading remem-
bered speeches of Freddie Bartholomew or C. Aubrey Smith,
and it was all very uproarious and, on his side, brilliant; but
what brings that half-hour repeatedly to my memory is the un-
remitted misery that was in his eyes. Once, a number of us left
a dinner party given by F. O. Matthiessen, at which Dylan had
been delightful and ghastly, and went to Cambridge for a se-
quence of nightcaps at my apartment; something was played on
the phonograph for a long while, and for a long while Dylan
whirled round and round the room, all alone, like a joyless tee-
totum; then he collapsed on the couch, between my wife and
Betty Eberhart, sobbing that he was a bottle-shaped monster,
neither man nor woman, and a phony, written-out poet soon to
be exposed as such.

Moments of that sort need to be remembered, both for the
truth's sake and in reproof of false accusers. It was not heartless

American entrepreneurs and wicked professors' martinis that did Dylan in; one could cheer him and take care of him up to a point, but he was finally uncontrollable and unhappy. For the most part, in his company, you had a choice between worrying to no purpose or having a drink and enjoying him.

He was fine company. I found him much more literary, and even scholarly, than his enthusiasts generally wanted him to be. But that was not the most of it. It is a pity that memoirs of Thomas so seldom give any idea of his gaudy banter, his storytelling, his power of mimicry, his Chaplinesque clowning—and I reproach myself for lacking the gift to do so here. He had gusto, and was the cause of gusto in others. Four or five of us once drove directly from his reading at Brandeis University to the nearest bar, and, while I was parking the car, Dylan and my wife went in as an advance party and claimed a booth. When the waitress appeared, the two said grandly, spontaneously, and in concert, "TWELVE BEERS." The girl brought them unblinkingly. As we left the bar that night, it was necessary to talk Dylan out of leaving a disproportionate amount of his Brandeis fee as a tip for the waitress.

Of too many possible recollections, I want to end with one which also has to do with an aspect of his generosity. By the time Dylan was making a second round of the country, we were living in Lincoln, a half-hour's drive from my office at Harvard. One evening, Dylan did a splendid job of booming and intoning at Lincoln's De Cordova Museum, after which he was asked to a small gathering at the house of one of the sponsors. The Lincoln people present were attractive, intelligent, and lively, but obviously not given to hell-raising. Because they were amiable people (also, I think, because Lincoln was our town and these our neighbors), the Thomases drank little and were, as I recall the occasion, outrageously seemly. Caitlin sat straight in her chair, with a dancer's good back, and spoke, among other things, of the merits of different oysters. Dylan was amusing as always, yet hearing him rumble affably about the weather as if he were entertaining the vicar, I thought I glimpsed in him the "genteel" person whom his more boisterous self felt the need to outrage. But tonight there was no outrage, no scene, no smashing of anything; all was amazing propriety until we were out on the dark driveway amidst the cars, and I foolishly offered a last drink at our place, and the quarreling began.

2

The following was written as a little preface for the full score of Leonard Bernstein's Candide, *which was published by Boosey and Hawkes in 1994.*

Working with Lenny on *Candide,* I sometimes felt a certain territorial anxiety. I couldn't read or write music, but he could read books, played a mean game of anagrams, and was exceedingly quick and clever with words. I feared that I couldn't afford a writer's block, lest this very literate composer grow impatient and write my lyrics for me. Once, over luncheon with him and Lillian Hellman, I paraded my literacy by quoting some little-known lines from Lewis Carroll's *Sylvie and Bruno;* whereupon Lenny, to my distress, completed the quotation. But there was, on the whole, no need to be protective of my verbal domain; in our planning and making of numbers, Lenny did his best to rein in his versatility, and we had an agreeable division of labor.

Where we most collaborated on language was in the making of dummy lyrics, and that was always great fun. In cases where existing music was to be furnished with words, we often devised nonsensical verses which, embodying the music's rhythms in words of a sort, might bring me a little closer to the pertinent verbalizing of Lenny's sound and movement. On one occasion, for example, it occurred to us that a tune which Lenny had composed for the birthday of his son, Alexander, might serve for a number about Candide's departure from Buenos Aires in Act II. The tune—Lenny called it a species of schottische—was tripping and animated in the extreme, and it was therefore especially necessary for me to grope toward some verbal equivalent by way of a provisional or "dummy" lyric. The reader may be amused to know that the lyric of "Bon Voyage," in its dummy stage, began with these asinine lines:

> *Oh, what a lovely villager!*
> *Oh, what a lovely, lovely villager bird!*

People who question me about my work with Lenny are forever saying, "But you must have quarreled sometimes." Of course we did, though neither of us had an aptitude for stormy wrangling. I recall a day when, having differed about some number or other, we were sitting, mute and unhappy, in his studio at Lambert's Cove. After some minutes of silence, I began, quite unconsciously, to whistle. "Do you know what you're whistling?" Lenny exclaimed. "It's '*Pace, Pace*' from *Forza*! Oh," he went on, "how I envy that man's melodic inventiveness, and the way he could make something powerful out of the simplest jump-rope tune!" He moved to the piano and played Verdi's great aria, and before he was through we had quite forgotten ourselves, and our little differences, and were ready to get to work again.

Lenny's music for *Candide* seems to me perpetually fresh and exciting, and I am happy to have been part of an enterprise which prompted it.

3

Here is an excerpt from a letter to Tom Clark, biographer of the poet Charles Olson, who had requested information about Olson's visits to his alma mater, Wesleyan.

Back in the sixties, Wesleyan had many poetry readings and poetry festivals. In part, this was because the Wesleyan University Press had decided to initiate a poetry program, and in its first decade (1959–69) was bringing out many excellent books by poets of many persuasions; as a spin-off of that program, many public readings were sponsored by the Press. Another reason for the phenomenon was George Garrett, a poet and member of the English Department, who had a talent for planning poetry festivals and for securing the necessary funds.

I first met Charlie Olson during one of Wesleyan's festivals, at a cocktail party given by Ray Flynn, director of the Press. Though the Flynns' living room was packed with standing and chattering people, it was easy to locate Olson because of his six-foot-nine stature, and I soon was talking with him. He was hearty and friendly. What I remember of our conversation (which was difficult to conduct in the party bedlam) is that he recalled a critical article of the late forties in which he and I were characterized as emergent leaders of emergent poetic schools; he greeted me, in other words, as a coach or quarterback might greet the coach or quarterback of a rival team. There was no implication that my school of poetry was a wrong or misguided school; he was more generous about that than I have known some other Black Mountain poets to be; but it was clear that he *did* think in terms of rival schools and aesthetics.

Often, during Wesleyan's "festival" period, reading programs were divided between two or more readers: Charlie was to read, on the occasion I have been recalling, for the second half of an hour, following a half-hour's reading by Hyam Plutzik, one of WUP's authors. Some of Olson's friends and admirers (Robert Duncan, Norman O. Brown, and others) felt that it was insulting to Olson that he be asked to share a program, and to read for so short a time. During Plutzik's reading, this pro-Olson claque produced, in the back rows of the audience, sounds of muffled mockery. Charlie's reading consisted in great part of false starts: he would say, "The lordly and isolate Satyrs . . ." and then stop, apparently unsatisfied with the rhythm he had given to the words; he would stand and think for a time and then try it again; and again. Fortunately he was able, before time ran out, to satisfy himself as to the right rhythmic attack for his variations on Rimbaud, which I much enjoyed hearing. Because the atmosphere of the sixties favored eccentricity, some of the audience relished the unconventionality of Olson's performance, but there was also rather a bit of disappointment. My recollection is that, after the reading, Olson gave another and longer reading at the house of N. O. Brown, this time to a group of his supporters.

The next day I encountered Olson in the student cafeteria, and he invited me to go out (with a bottle of whiskey) to pay a call on his old mentor Wilbert Snow. Bill declined the offer of a drink, Olson and I sipped temperately, and we had a long and pleasant and rambling talk in Bill's living room. When Bill found that Charlie had not read Frost for years, he asked me to read aloud "Home Burial." Olson said that he had forgotten how good Frost could be, and also remarked that the poem was an expression of "scarcity." That remark remained mysterious, though Bill and I urged him to clarify it; it seemed to have something to do with the poverty of the people in the poem.

Later, Bill and I got going excitedly about Keats, and Charlie, having listened for a time, said, "Do you know what you guys are talking about? Subject matter!" Subject matter, I suppose, as opposed to poetic form. It amused me that, since Bill and I were classified in the sixties as traditional formalists, Charlie should reproach us for discussing words and themes rather than poetic structure. Throughout our visit, I was struck by Olson's gracious, warm, and filial behavior toward Snow.

On a later occasion, Olson came to Wesleyan to read his poems at Alpha Delta Phi, as part of the fraternity's lecture series. I don't want to sound censorious, but it was a ghastly performance. The water carafe on the table next to the lectern may or may not have contained gin, but in any case Charlie *had* been drinking. He read very little; he strode about, haranguing the audience (and individuals in the audience) about such matters as Awareness of Topography; he repeatedly crossed himself for no apparent reason; it was not a good show. Though many of his hearers were theoretically impatient of "structured" and "establishment" behavior, Olson alienated the entire audience. One slightly annoyed professor said to me, as we were leaving, that he had known Charlie well at Harvard. In those days, the professor said, Charlie had been as coherent as any other graduate student; the professor regretted that Charlie had since made a deliberate decision to be inarticulate.

4

Stanley Burnshaw wrote me in January of 1984, when he was working on his memoir Robert Frost Himself, *to ask whether Frost had not, despite his "reputed dislike of any competition," been friendly and encouraging toward me. In the first paragraph of my reply, I made ignorant excuses for*

*Lawrance Thompson, having read too little of Thompson's
Frost biography to know the extent of his malignity.*

Dear Stanley Burnshaw,

I'm slow to read biographies of poets I have known, the lit-
erary life being sufficiently claustrophobic without rehashing
everything; but I did read some of Thompson's books on Robert,
and have gained some sense of what I left unread. The stress
on RF's worser aspects was fairly predictable, I think; Frost and
some of his advocates had long given the public the impression
that he was all mellow wisdom and gruff kindliness, and from
the late forties on I continually heard (especially at Bread Loaf,
sometimes in Cambridge) truth-lovers insisting upon his darker
side. Bill Sloan once said to me, "Dick, you'll never be a great
poet because you're not enough of a bastard; the great ones are
bastards like Robert." Thompson may have had reason for ani-
mus, but my guess is that he was chiefly motivated by a desire
to right the balance and acknowledge Frost's less mellow
qualities.... Unfortunately, Thompson's correction of the bal-
ance had the effect—so I thought in reading what I read—of
minimizing the generosity that was in RF's nature. But all this,
of course, you know.

Like many others, I had opportunities to see RF's extreme
competitiveness in action. Amongst Harvard people, he would
often reminisce about the English literary scene as he'd en-
countered it, busily and hilariously undermining such major fig-
ures as Yeats and Pound, and saying that F. S. Flint had been
a more vital force in poetry than either. Of such whittling at
other reputations there was much always. Yet it seems to me
that there was always more generosity than the righters-of-the-
balance allowed. He was a good friend to John Holmes, and
provided a blurb for one of Holmes' earlier books; he was a

friend also to Robert Francis, over many years. As you mention, he took considerable interest in the work of Roethke and Lowell—though he could criticize them sharply for indulging their imbalances (as he saw it), and for admitting "craziness" into their poems. It strikes me that his benevolence toward younger poets increased as he grew older. He had a warm relationship with Bill Meredith. I don't know whether he knew Howard Nemerov's poetry well (Kay Morrison once told me that she couldn't get Robert to keep up with the good work of his juniors), but I remember his telling me during his last illness that he liked Howard and "admired his personal austerity." I'm sure that I could think of other instances in which he opened up toward poets who were not sycophantic "minor birds" but writers of genuine stature.

As for myself—which is what you asked me about—I had an initial advantage with RF because my wife's great-aunt, Susan Hayes Ward, was by RF's testimony the "first friend of his poetry," while her grandfather, William Hayes Ward, had published RF's poem "My Butterfly" in the New York *Independent*. I don't know when he first looked at my work; I never forced anything on him. Early on, he said the only slighting thing ever reported to me. Avis DeVoto asked him, at Bread Loaf, how he liked my poems, and he reportedly said, "What kind of poems would you expect from a good-looking tennis player?" I was glad of the "good-looking," but not gratified by what he seemed to be saying. Not long after, however, he said to me at Dartmouth of my poem "The Puritans" that "it was the best little poem he'd seen in a year or so." And a bit later (1950 or so, I should guess), he suggested to Louis Untermeyer that I be included in the next edition of his anthology. Louis later told me about that. He had not, he said, read any of my work at the time of RF's recommendation, and he did not then take the suggestion seriously, because he felt that the competitive Robert would never recommend any poet who might ultimately deprive him of anthology space. My last two stories are, I think, additional proof that RF *could* encourage a younger poet and go out of his way to further his fortunes. We saw RF often during the rest of his life, visiting him at Ripton and in Cambridge, having him for dinner or as a house-guest in Cambridge or in Portland, Connecticut. It was always good. Once or twice he snapped at me; once or twice I sassed him and was not banished for it; those things are consistent with friendship. As I have told elsewhere—in an interview, I think—there was a day when I was walking away from RF's cabin in Ripton and he called me back to say something like, "I just wanted to say that we're friends, aren't we?" For a man so indisposed to gush as he was, that seemed a considerable display of warmth.

I've doubtless answered your enquiry at greater length than you bargained for, but I sympathize with your wish to *re*-right the balance, and wished to give as much evidence as came to mind. My opening remark about "rehashing" does not apply, of course, to your memoir-in-progress, which I look forward to reading. . . .

PS: My wife has looked over this letter, and she offers some additions-and-corrections. She says that RF read my first book in Cambridge in 1947 or 1948, and telephoned her to speak well of it. In a later year, when RF was staying with us in Portland, she and RF had a talk into the wee hours, I having gone to bed because I had to teach the next morning. In the course of it, RF again spoke approvingly of my work, and told Charlee that she must "take good care of me, and not let me go crazy." He said that he had always fought to avoid the mental instability that was part of his inheritance (as of mine). I add this postscript not to underline RF's endorsement of me, but as further evidence that he could praise and be solicitous.

Elizabeth Bishop

MY WIFE and I first met Elizabeth Bishop at the Richard Eberharts' apartment in Cambridge, more than thirty years ago. She had just recently published her first book, *North and South*, which the reviewers had admired but which had also had the rarer fate of being instantly precious to many of her fellow poets, who rightly saw it as something new, distinguished, and inexhaustibly fresh. The woman we met that evening was not a literary figure, and was clearly not embarked on anything so pompous and public as a career. She was quiet, comely, friendly, amusing, and amusable; she spoke in a modest and somewhat murmuring way, often asking questions as if she expected us Cantabrigians to have the answers. But in matters of importance to her she turned out to have quite definite answers of her own. For example, she told me that Poe's best poem, for her taste, was a little-known piece called "Fairy-Land." Years of rereading that poem have brought me close to her opinion, and have led me to see that her fondness for it was based on a true affinity. "Fairy-Land" is a charming dream-vision, written in a transparent style unusual for Poe; at the same time, its weeping trees and multitudinous moons are repeatedly and humorously challenged by the voice of common sense; out of which conflict the poem somehow modulates, at the close, into a poignant yearning for transcendence. All of the voices of that poem have their counterparts in Elizabeth's own work.

Reticent as she was, Elizabeth Bishop wrote several autobiographical pieces in which she testified to a lifelong sense of dislocation. That is, she missed from the beginning what some enjoy, an unthinking conviction that things ought to be as they are; that one ought to exist, bearing a certain name; that the school-bus driver should have a fox terrier; that there should be a red hydrant down at the corner; that it all makes sense. Her short prose masterpiece, "In the Village," is quite simply an account of how, in childhood, her confidence in the world's plausibility and point was shaken. Behind the story lies her father's death in the first year of her life; hanging over the story, in the Nova Scotian sky, is the scream of her mother, who was forever lost to the child through an emotional breakdown. Here are two resonant sentences from the story, having to do with the sending of family packages to her mother. "The address of the sanitarium is in my grandmother's handwriting, in purple indelible pencil, on smoothed-out wrapping paper. It will never come off."

If the world is a strange place, then it readily shades into dream. So many of Elizabeth's poems take place at the edge of sleep, or on the threshold of waking, lucidly fusing two orders of consciousness. Some of them are written out of remembered dreams. And then there are superb poems like "The Man-Moth," in which a tragic sensibility is portrayed *under the form* of dream. In a later poem, "The Riverman," her capacity for navigating the irrational enabled her to enter the mind of a witch-doctor, and to visit the water-spirits of the Amazon. All this has little to do with the influence of French surrealism, I think; as her Robinson Crusoe says of his artifacts in *Geography III*, Elizabeth Bishop's poems are "home-made."

In another kind of poem, she sets some part of the world before her and studies it with a describing eye, an interrogating mind, and a personality eager for coherence. This is the kind of poem, written in a style at once natural and lapidary, in which her stunning accuracies of perception and comparison make us think of her friend and early encourager, Marianne Moore. A sandy beach "hisses like fat"; she sees on a wall "the mildew's ignorant map"; on a gusty day in Washington she notes how "Unceasingly, the little flags/ Feed their limp stripes into the air." One could go on quoting such felicities forever, and it is such things which have led the critics to use the words *wit, delight, precision, elegance,* and *fastidiousness;* at the same time, her descriptive genius has led some to say that her poetry is a poetry of surfaces. At moments she seems to have felt this herself, as when, at the close of her poem "The Armadillo," she grows suddenly impatient of the prettiness of poetry and speaks in italics of fear and pain. But in fact her poems, for all their objectivity, are much involved in what they see: though she seldom protests, or specifies her emotions, her work is full of an implicit compassion, and her friend Robert Lowell justly ascribed to her a tone "of large, grave tenderness and sorrowing amusement."

That expression "sorrowing amusement" is wonderfully exact, and of course it would be quite wrong to overstress the sorrow part of it. If she was afflicted by the absurdity of things, she also took delight in everything curious, incongruous, or crazy; that's one reason why she was the best of company. Almost all of my mental pictures of her belong somewhere on a scale between amiability and hilarity; and we have one real picture, a snapshot in which, with the fiercest of expressions, she is about to use my head as a croquet ball.

When she looked in her poetry for ultimate answers, she generally expressed the search in the key of geography, of travel. And she always reported that such answers were undiscoverable. In the poem "Cape Breton" she says, "Whatever the landscape had of meaning appears to have been abandoned." In "Arrival at Santos," she mocks the tourist with his "immodest demands for a different world,/ And a better life, and complete comprehension/ of both at last," and concludes with the intensely ironic line, "We are driving to the interior." In another poem about travel, she regrets that so many sights in Rome or Mexico or Marrakesh have failed to make a pattern, that everything has been "only connected by 'and' and 'and'." She wishes that some revelation, some Nativity scene, might have brought all into focus. In and out of her poetry, she lamented her want of a comprehensive philosophy; yet I cannot be sorry that so honest a nature as hers refused to force itself into a system, and I question whether system is the only way to go deep into things.

Though she had no orthodox convictions, and wondered at such certainties in others, Elizabeth Bishop had religious concerns and habits of feeling. I think of her poem about St. Peter; I think of the "pure and angelic note" of the blacksmith's hammer in her story "In the Village," and the way that story ends with the cry, "O, beautiful sound, strike again!" I think of the fact that when she was asked to make a selection of someone's poems for a poetry newsletter, she came up with an anthology of hymns. (Her favorite hymn, by the way, was the Easter one which begins, "Come ye faithful, raise the strain/ Of triumphant gladness.") Above all, I think of her poem called "Twelfth Morning": it is a poem about Epiphany, the day when things are manifested, and its opening lines say:

> Like a first coat of whitewash when it's wet,
> the thin grey mist lets everything show through...

One thing that comes through the mist is a sound from the shore, the sound of "the sandpipers'/ heart-broken cries," and that I take for a sign that grief is a radical presence in the world.

But there is also another phenomenon, a black boy named Balthazár who bears the name of one of the Magi, and on whose head is a four-gallon can which "keeps flashing that the world's a pearl." The vision of Balthazár and his four-gallon pearl is qualified by amusement; nevertheless it is a vision. It seems to me that Elizabeth Bishop's poetry perceives beauty as well as absurdity, exemplifies the mind's power to make beauty, and embodies compassion; though her world is ultimately mysterious, one of its constants is sorrow, and another is some purity or splendor which, though forever defiled, is also, as her poem "Anaphora" says, perpetually renewed.

This appreciation has been too literary, with too little of the personal in it. Elizabeth herself would not have been guilty of such disproportion. She attended to her art, but she also attended to other people and to the things of every day. James Merrill put this happily, in a recent reminiscence, when he spoke of her "lifelong impersonation of an ordinary woman." Well, she was an incomparable poet and a delectable person; we loved her very much.

At a 1993 celebration of Elizabeth Bishop in Key West, some
of the poets present (James Merrill, Anthony Hecht, and I)
read their poems in her honor, and each began by reading
and appreciating some poem of hers. Here is what I said
about one of the poems of North and South.

On "Little Exercise"

LITTLE EXERCISE

Think of the storm roaming the sky uneasily
like a dog looking for a place to sleep in,
listen to it growling.

Think how they must look now, the mangrove keys
lying out there unresponsive to the lightning
in dark, coarse-fibred families,

where occasionally a heron may undo his head,
shake up his feathers, make an uncertain comment
when the surrounding water shines.

Think of the boulevard and the little palm trees
all stuck in rows, suddenly revealed
as fistfuls of limp fish-skeletons.

It is raining there. The boulevard
and its broken sidewalks with weeds in every crack,
are relieved to be wet, the sea to be freshened.

Now the storm goes away again in a series
of small, badly lit battle-scenes,
each in "Another part of the field."

Think of someone sleeping in the bottom of a row-boat
tied to a mangrove root or the pile of a bridge;
think of him as uninjured, barely disturbed.

FRANK BIDART was right in asserting, at one of yesterday's sessions, that no poem of Elizabeth Bishop's is merely descriptive. To be sure, she often denounced herself in just those terms, and I can still hear her disconsolately saying of her work that it was "all description, no philosophy." But she did herself an injustice. And I was chagrined to discover, in preparing for this occasion, that I have been similarly unjust to a poem of hers for forty-some years—that I've cherished it, for all that time, without properly understanding it.

"Little Exercise" can be taken, and is generally taken, for a virtuoso piece which, by way of a number of brilliant similes or flash pictures, shows the reader (or some novice poet, perhaps) how to envision a subtropical thunderstorm. Nothing in the poem strongly resists that interpretation, unless it be that the final picture—the man in the boat—is less excitingly descriptive than the rest. What jarred me into a better understanding was the fact—which I came upon just two days ago—that the poem was originally published in *The New Yorker* under the title "Little Exercise: 4 A.M." To see the poem as happening at a particular time in the small hours, a time when people are often abed and alone, was to begin to recast it as a monodrama having something to say about fear and self-mastery.

Here is the plot of "Little Exercise," considered as a drama. In a dark Key West bedroom, at four in the morning, a great thunderclap awakens a woman who is timid about storms. Rather than give in to runaway fear, she commands her imagination to visualize the storm as it roams or flashes in the sky, and to picture the effects of rain and lightning on her familiar island and its outlying keys. The repeated imperative "Think" is addressed not to the reader but to the woman herself, as part of a little exercise in imaginative control—an exercise which confronts the reality of the storm with adequate words, and renders it ultimately harmless, even benign. By the end of the poem, the woman is as untroubled by lightning as the mangrove keys, as "relieved" as the cooling pavement of the boulevard, as "barely disturbed" as the man in the boat, and ready to sleep again.

Among the means by which the poem tames its storm are humor and the refusal of sublime scale. The latter tactic begins with the "little" of the title, and continues with the diminishing dog simile of the opening lines, the little palms of the boulevard, the insouciant focus on the weedy cracks in the sidewalk. A salient instance of humor is the wonderful verb in the phrase "a heron may undo his head." When "the storm goes away again in a series/ of small, badly-lit battle-scenes," the description is superbly accurate, yet at the same time it treats the storm both as "small" and as amusingly inept, like amateur theatricals.

But there is no need for such pointings-out, really. As soon as one ceases to view the poem as a descriptive exercise, and sees that it is a little drama of self-control, all matters of structure, strategy, and tone become quite clear.

The magazine Field *devoted part of its Fall 1981 issue to a celebration, by various hands, of the poet Robert Francis. This was my contribution.*

On Robert Francis' "Sheep"

SHEEP

From where I stand the sheep stand still
As stones against the stony hill.

The stones are gray
And so are they.

And both are weatherworn and round,
Leading the eye back to the ground.

Two mingled flocks—
The sheep, the rocks.

And still no sheep stirs from its place
Or lifts its Babylonian face.

I THINK THAT I have known this poem since my undergraduate days at Amherst, and I remain grateful for its perfection.

It is, if you look for tricks, a very artful poem indeed. Two motionless constellations of things—sheep and rocks—are being likened, and this is formally expressed by the linked twoness of tetrameter couplets, and of tetrameter broken in two to make dimeter couplets. By the time you get to the second line of the fourth couplet, a line which simply juxtaposes "The sheep, the rocks," there are two mirroring monometers within the dimeter measure.

The first line of the poem is the only one, to my ear, which remotely threatens to run over into the next; elsewhere, pauses and punctuation give an even balancing movement to each couplet, and so enforce the idea of parallelism. There is balance or mirroring, too, in the words and sounds of the poem, most obviously in the *stand/stand* and *stones/stony* of the first couplet, more subtly in the way the first line's *still* reappears all the way down in the last line but one.

Each of the couplets ends with a full stop, and the effect of these repeated arrests is to keep the idea of movement from getting started, to stress the idea of fixity.

All of this formal appropriateness (so pleasing to experience, so dry to hear about) is there in the poem, and yet in fact the poem does not seem tricky. Why not? For one thing, the language and word order are so plain and natural that the sheep and rocks seem almost unmediated. The reader has scarcely any sense of a poet standing between him and the scene, brandishing a rhetoric and offering clever interpretations. Because the poet thus effaces himself, because he writes so transparently, his formal felicities—though they have their effect—are not felt as part of a performance. The poem's first line—"From where I stand the sheep stand still"—very firmly begins this minimization of the poet's presence: it focuses the poem not on "I" but on the sheep, and it presents the poet not as a sensibility but as a mere locus or vantage point.

A final effect of that line, of course, is to convey a sense of a fixed scene fixedly viewed. The witness doesn't move any more than the stones or sheep do. However, the mind of the poet shapes and moves the poem far more than his plain manner lets on. Each of the first four couplets states some resemblance between the sheep and the rocks: their stillness, their grayness, their rondure and texture, their flocklike arrangement. These statements have a cumulative force, but it also strikes me that, beginning with the modest simile of the first couplet, they grow progressively stronger in nature, until stones and sheep are "mingled flocks," and the mirroring elements of the poem approach a state of fusion.

Fusion occurs in the word "Babylonian." In this poem, what a word! "Sheep" begins with ten successive monosyllables, but here at the end we meet a grand five-syllable word with a capital letter, a word which suddenly flies off beyond the poem's preserve toward something far and ancient, a word with none of the plainness of what has gone before it, a word in which the poem drops all pretense that it is not a product of imagination. The effect is explosive, and then there is an immediate double take as the reader sees that "Babylonian" is after all quite at home in this accurate poem, by reason of its evocative accuracy. The word asks us first, and most importantly, to combine sheep and stone by recalling Babylonian and Assyrian sculpture—in particular, I should think, those famous Assyrian bas-reliefs which represent men and animals in profile, and have a stylization of the hirsute which renders the sheep an ideal and frequent subject. The line "Leading the eye back to the ground" compels us, by the way, to see Francis' sheep in a side view, as if they were posing for a relief.

The faces of sheep do, in fact, suggest the physiognomies of Mesopotamia and the Near East, and I remember Umberto Saba's poem in which he describes *una capra dal viso semita,* a goat with a Semitic face. Finally, I believe, the poem asks us to think of how long—in the lands which the Bible mentions, and in others, and in unrecorded times and places—the sheep have been with us.

*When reading Victorian poetry under Douglas Bush at
Harvard, I was struck by the suggestive presences of Dante,
Milton, and Shakespeare in Tennyson's "Ulysses," and made
notes toward an essay about the matter. The essay got done
some fifty years later, when Robert Pack invited me to dis-
cuss some poem or other in his* Touchstones *(1995.)*

Tennyson's Voyage
of the Mind

ULYSSES

It little profits that an idle king,
By this still hearth, among these barren crags,
Matched with an aged wife, I mete and dole
Unequal laws unto a savage race,
That hoard, and sleep, and feed, and know not me.

I cannot rest from travel; I will drink
Life to the lees. All times I have enjoyed
Greatly, have suffered greatly, both with those
That loved me, and alone; on shore, and when
Through scudding drifts the rainy Hyades
Vexed the dim sea. I am become a name;
For always roaming with a hungry heart
Much have I seen and known—cities of men
And manners, climates, councils, governments,
Myself not least, but honored of them all—
And drunk delight of battle with my peers,
Far on the ringing plains of windy Troy.
I am a part of all that I have met;

Yet all experience is an arch wherethrough
Gleams that untraveled world whose margin fades
Forever and forever when I move.
How dull it is to pause, to make an end,
To rust unburnished, not to shine in use!
As though to breathe were life! Life piled on life
Were all too little, and of one to me
Little remains; but every hour is saved
From that eternal silence, something more,
A bringer of new things; and vile it were
For some three suns to store and hoard myself,
And this gray spirit yearning in desire
To follow knowledge like a sinking star,
Beyond the utmost bound of human thought.

This is my son, mine own Telemachus,
To whom I leave the scepter and the isle—
Well-loved of me, discerning to fulfill
This labor, by slow prudence to make mild
A rugged people, and through soft degrees
Subdue them to the useful and the good.
Most blameless is he, centered in the sphere
Of common duties, decent not to fail
In offices of tenderness, and pay
Meet adoration to my household gods,
When I am gone. He works his work, I mine.

There lies the port; the vessel puffs her sail;
There gloom the dark, broad seas. My mariners,
Souls that have toiled, and wrought, and thought with me—
That ever with a frolic welcome took
The thunder and the sunshine, and opposed

Free hearts, free foreheads—you and I are old;
Old age hath yet his honor and his toil.
Death closes all; but something ere the end,
Some work of noble note, may yet be done,
Not unbecoming men that strove with Gods.
The lights begin to twinkle from the rocks;
The long day wanes; the slow moon climbs; the deep
Moans round with many voices. Come, my friends,
'Tis not too late to seek a newer world.
Push off, and sitting well in order smite
The sounding furrows; for my purpose holds
To sail beyond the sunset, and the baths
Of all the western stars, until I die.
It may be that the gulfs will wash us down;
It may be we shall touch the Happy Isles,
And see the great Achilles, whom we knew.
Though much is taken, much abides; and though
We are not now that strength which in old days
Moved earth and heaven, that which we are, we are—
One equal temper of heroic hearts,
Made weak by time and fate, but strong in will
To strive, to seek, to find, and not to yield.

ULYSSES HEARS "many voices" in the beckoning deep, and in this complex and celebrated soliloquy there are also many voices—diverse tones, moods, assertions, and echoes which the reader is challenged to hear rightly, and to attune if he can. To be sure, a poem so handsomely written can easily be plundered for simple messages: Robert Kennedy, campaigning for the Presidency, was given to quoting " 'Tis not too late to seek a newer world"; that phrase and others are dear to commencement speakers, while "Old age hath yet his honor and his toil" has proven useful with maturer audiences. Tennyson himself tells us that "Ulysses" may securely be taken as a heartening poem written at a time of grief and despondency. It was begun a few days after the death of his dearest friend, Arthur Hallam, whom he (and others) had regarded as a young man of "high speculative endowments," capable of addressing the intellectual and spiritual problems of the age. It was "written under the sense of loss," Tennyson said, "and gave my feeling about the need of going forward, and braving the struggle of life."

Certainly the salient echoes of the first thirty-odd lines support the idea of getting on with it, of rousing oneself to action. The "sleep, and feed" of line 5 has reminded scholars of a soliloquy of Hamlet's:

> *How all occasions do inform against me*
> *And spur my dull revenge! What is a man,*
> *If the chief good and market of his time*
> *Be but to sleep and feed? A beast, no more.*
> *Sure he that made us with such large discourse,*
> *Looking before and after, gave us not*
> *That capability and godlike reason*
> *To fust in us unused....*
>
> *(IV, iv)*

The sound and sense of that last phrase may also have helped to prompt lines 22–23 of "Ulysses:"

> *How dull it is to pause, to make an end,*
> *To rust unburnished, not to shine in use!*

The same two lines have reminded me and others of Shakespeare's own Ulysses, in *Troilus and Cressida*, urging Achilles not to rest upon his laurels:

> *Perseverance, dear my lord,*
> *Keeps honor bright; to have done, is to hang*
> *Quite out of fashion, like a rusty mail,*
> *In monumental mockery.*
>
> *(III, iii, 150ff.)*

In what it says and in what it echoes, the forepart of
Tennyson's poem is largely the soliloquy of a heroic spirit be-
stirring itself to further adventure; we rightly respond to Ulysses'
great appetite for life, and to such splendid measures as "Far
on the ringing plains of windy Troy." And yet the first five lines
of the poem, which Tennyson latterly printed as a discrete para-
graph, are the musings not of a hero but of a depressed island
ruler who is weary of his faithful Penelope, contemptuous of
his people, and too bored and lazy to improve the laws which
he administers. Such attitudes cannot be appealing in a poem
by Tennyson, who by 1833 was already becoming the poet of
duty and social responsibility, and they jar as well with the ex-
pectations of Ulysses which we derive from Homer's *Odyssey*.
But in fact the *Odyssey* is not the main and formative source of
"Ulysses," which in many respects is inconsistent with Homer;
for instance, if Tiresias prophesies in Homer's Book XI that
Ulysses, having regained his home and beloved queen, must set
forth on yet another journey, it is an inland journey, from which
he will return to die "after a rich old age, surrounded by a happy
people."

Tennyson's version of Ulysses is chiefly based upon the 26th
canto of Dante's *Inferno*, where Ulysses—the wily deviser of the
Trojan horse—is found among those who, by deceit and by
counseling others to deceive, have misused the high faculty of
reason. Ulysses tells, in a long and beautiful speech, how on

leaving Circe's island he exhorted his companions, saying, "Consider what you were born to: you were not made to live like brutes, but to pursue excellence and knowledge"; and how he sailed with them then, in a "foolish flight" (*folle volo*) through the Pillars of Hercules toward a final engulfment in the South Atlantic. "Neither fondness for my son," his narrative begins, "nor piety toward my old father, nor the due love that should have comforted Penelope, could conquer in me the yearning to know the world entire, and the good and evil ways of men."

Tennyson's poem begins also with Ulysses' culpable rejections and forsakings, and then—despite a pompous frequency of "me" and "I" unmatched except by Milton's Satan—becomes more attractive, more positive, more vigorous, more eloquent as the hero recalls his past adventures and consolidates his will to go voyaging again. That the second paragraph is self-persuasive rather than fully resolved, we know by certain negative overtones which seem almost like slips of the tongue. "Yet all experience is an arch wherethrough/ Gleams that untraveled world whose margin fades/ Forever and forever when I move" is a way of saying that much remains to be seen; yet the weariness of "Forever and forever" seems to grant that the quest for final knowledge is vain, and that (as the voice of despair whispers in "The Two Voices") the aged seeker is doomed to "seem to find, but still to seek." The words "To follow knowledge like a sinking star," however one may parse them, have disastrous implications in a voyage-poem, and make the reader ask whether Ulysses is seeking or fleeing, and whether his goal is renewed "life" or suicide. The reader must try, I think, to conceive a troubled, wavering Ulysses of whom all those things might be true.

Up to this halfway point, Ulysses has been 1) expressing disgust at his life in Ithaca, and 2) talking himself into a last embarcation; now, as I read the poem, he imagines what he will say to the leading citizens of Ithaca when he abdicates and embarks. His tone accordingly grows politic, measured, and reassuringly colorless. There is none of the gruff dismissiveness of the poem's opening lines; the savage Ithacans, those beastly sleepers and feeders, are now merely "rugged," and Ulysses speaks with some affection of Telemachus, though condescending toward his son's merely "blameless" and "decent" capacities. In a poem responsive to the loss of Arthur Hallam, who had he lived might have been "A life in civic action warm,/ A soul on highest mission sent,/ A potent voice in Parliament,/ A pillar steadfast in the storm," Ulysses' low regard for governance and public service, though understandable in a restless hero of action, is not in itself to be admired.

In the closing paragraph of the poem, Ulysses imagines or rehearses what he will say to his mariners—how he will enlist them in a *folle volo* beyond the set limits of the known world. Homer's Odysseus returned alone to Ithaca, having lost all his companions, but Tennyson provides his hero with sailors who are veterans of Troy. Ulysses can thus magnificently appeal to their heroic memories, as he has earlier done to his own, and thereby impress them into his service. At the same time, his inspiring speech is once more peppered with discordant notes. As Christopher Ricks has brilliantly pointed out, Ulysses' discourse, though urging departure for a "newer world," exhibits a weird and near-total avoidance of the future tense. "Gloom," "dark," moaning waters, swooning rhythms, and the phrase "until I die," hint once again at a morbid wish for death. And a number of phrases, such as "strove with Gods," evoke not only Troy but Milton's war in Heaven, and prepare us for a final sinister echo of Satan's "And courage never to submit or yield." (*Paradise Lost*, I, line 108.)

It may be that some of the dissonances in "Ulysses" belong not to Tennyson's portrait of his hero but to his own inclination to be sad, slow, and sonorous regardless of the subject. I think, nonetheless, that we can derive from the poem a vivid, intelligible personality who has the vices of his virtues. Ulysses is nobly eloquent, and he is also a crafty spellbinder; he is both great-hearted and egotistical; he loves bracing adventure, and is a shirker of "common duties"; he vigorously defies old age, and yet is depressed; he loves life and is sick of it; he is fearless but suicidal. We are left, however, with two uncertainties about him. The first is this: how far are we instructed to condemn this Ulysses, seeing that he is based on a damned soul in the *Inferno*, and puts us in mind of Satan's rhetoric in Hell? In the second place, though Ulysses is clearly not some globe-trotting retiree, what sort of "knowledge" is he sailing after, what sort of "thought" does he share with his shipmates, how will he use the reason which distinguishes him from brute beasts, and what "work of noble note" is he likely to accomplish? The answers to these questions only come, I think, when we change our focus and see "Ulysses" as an allegory of the bereaved Tennyson's resolution to ponder man's place in Nature, God's purpose in the world, our grounds for faith, our hope of immortality—great questions raised by Hallam's death, which Hallam (had he lived) might have illuminated for his time and society.

This is a poem about thinking—not the sort of thinking that deals in received ideas, and concerns itself with "common duties" and "household gods," but the kind that Wordsworth meant when he spoke of Newton as "a mind forever/ Voyaging through strange seas of thought, alone." Jung has said in our century that "all consciousness separates," and Hannah Arendt has written of the riskiness of philosophic thought, which withdraws from the senses, from action, and from the world. But on

the whole our day sees little danger in estranging mental ad-
venture, and we have to be reminded that earlier ages were wary
of it. Just before he tells of his encounter with the burning
shade of Ulysses, Dante says, "I sorrowed then, and sorrow now
again, when I direct my memory to what I saw; and more than
usually do I rein in my poetic genius, lest it run where Virtue
does not guide it." W. H. Auden is right, I believe, in saying
that Dante sees Ulysses, the foolhardy voyager, as succumbing
to "the concupiscence of curiosity," and reins in his own mind
lest he likewise be tempted to *libido sciendi.*

From Christian tradition, from his own conservative nature,
and from a family history full of brooding and aberration,
Tennyson would have understood Dante's fear of unbridled
thought and enquiry. The poet who had his Tithonus say

> *Why should a man desire in any way*
> *To vary from the kindly race of men,*
> *Or pass beyond the goal of ordinance*
> *Where all should pause, as is most meet for all?*

was not an enthusiast of overreaching. He would understand
the angel Raphael's rebuking Adam for his abstruse question-
ings of God's order—

> *Solicit not thy thoughts with matters hid,*
> *Leave them to God above, him serve and fear . . .*

—and Adam's enlightened response:

> *. . . apt the Mind or Fancy is to rove*
> *Uncheckt, and of her roving is no end;*
> *Till warn'd, or by experience taught, she learn*
> *That not to know at large of things remote*

> *From use, obscure and subtle, but to know*
> *That which before us lies in daily life,*
> *Is the prime Wisdom . . .*
>
> (PL, *VIII*)

He would further have understood the angel Uriel's saying, in Book III, that there is no excess in searching the works and ways of God, so long as the purpose of such searching is "to glorify/ The great Work-Master." Here is but one of many possible quotations in which Tennyson may be seen as agreeing with Dante and Milton:

> *Make knowledge circle with the winds;*
> *But let her herald, Reverence, fly*
> *Before her to whatever sky*
> *Bear seed of men and growth of minds.*
>
> *("Love Thou Thy Land," 1833–34)*

One might also put in evidence the prologue of *In Memoriam*, stanzas 5–8, and section CXIV *in toto*.

"Ulysses" is a poem which knows that speculative thinking about ultimate things entails some spiritual risk; and it is a poem which intends to speculate, come Hell or high water. It shakes off all misgivings and sets out after faraway truth, refusing the bonds and bounds of Virtue, Wisdom, Reverence. That bold resolve best accounts, I think, for the poem's flavor of defiance, and its occasional whiff of brimstone. These dangerous elements are counterbalanced by lines 63–64—

> *It may be we shall touch the Happy Isles,*
> *And see the great Achilles, whom we knew . . .*

—in which there is an implicit hope that Tennyson's intellectual quest will be justified. The critic John Pettigrew thinks it possible that "the Happy Isles, the dwelling of the virtuous after death, suggest a goal of renewed life in opposition to the gulfs" of line 62; I think that a certainty. It seems safe to identify Achilles with Hallam, as most readers do, and to infer that if Tennyson's mental journey should in some sense attain to Hallam, now a soul in bliss, he would then be acquitted of presumption, preserved from error, and put in possession of higher truths. Under the guise of Achilles, Hallam thus figures as the Beatrice of "Ulysses."

Between 1833 and 1849, Tennyson wrote many lyrics in memory of Arthur Hallam and in search of answers to the large issues raised by his friend's death. Arranged then into a loose unity, and published in 1850 as *In Memoriam A.H.H.*, these poems are his finest accomplishment (though finer in feeling than in thought) and may in retrospect be identified with the "work of noble note" of which "Ulysses" speaks. Section CIII of *In Memoriam* looks back to "Ulysses" in such a way as both to illuminate it and to revise it. What we have in CIII is a pageant-like dream-vision in which, as the poet himself explained, Tennyson voyages down the river of Life, accompanied by maiden-mariners who symbolize poetic and artistic powers—"all that make life beautiful here, which we hope will pass with us beyond the grave." As they draw near the sea (of death and afterlife), the poet and his maidens grow in size, strength, and grace, and soon, upon the deep, they see "A great ship lift her shining sides."

> *The man we loved was there on deck,*
> *But thrice as large as man he bent*

> *To greet us. Up the side I went,*
> *And fell in silence on his neck. . . .*

The vision obviously affirms the immortality of the soul;
Hallam's size expresses Tennyson's view of him as a precursor
of "that great race which is to be"—a much improved human
species; and, since Tennyson had come to see our spiritual de-
velopment as continuing in afterlife, the maidens are asked on
board:

> *And while the wind began to sweep*
> *A music out of sheet and shroud*
> *We steered her toward a crimson cloud*
> *That landlike slept along the deep.*

Section CIII is a happy dream, and has none of the ambiguity
of Ulysses' nature, none of the doubtfulness and defiance of his
contemplated journey. But it may help to confirm our sense of
an allegorical dimension in the earlier poem, letting us see what
sort of thought the mariners share, what sort of knowledge is
sought, and how a reunion in the Happy Isles might vindicate
and crown the expedition.

Michael McCurdy's Penmaen Press produced in 1979 an edition of Poe's tale "Eleonora." It was done in 264 copies for the Print Club of Cleveland, and contained a wood engraving by Fritz Eichenberg. I was asked to write a little introduction, which I shall present here as an afterword to the brief story itself.

Edgar Allan Poe's Eleonora

Sub conservatione formae specificae salva anima.
—RAYMOND LULLY

I AM COME of a race noted for vigor of fancy and ardor of passion. Men have called me mad; but the question is not yet settled, whether madness is or is not the loftiest intelligence —whether much that is glorious—whether all that is profound—does not spring from disease of thought—from *moods* of mind exalted at the expense of the general intellect. They who dream by day are cognizant of many things which escape those who dream only by night. In their grey visions they obtain glimpses of eternity, and thrill, in awaking, to find that they have been upon the verge of the great secret. In snatches, they learn something of the wisdom which is of good, and more of the mere knowledge which is of evil. They penetrate, however rudderless or compassless, into the vast ocean of the "light ineffable," and again, like the adventurers of the Nubian geographer, *"agressi sunt mare tenebrarum, quid in eo esset exploraturi."*

We will say, then, that I am mad. I grant, at least, that there are two distinct conditions of my mental existence—the condition of a lucid reason, not to be disputed, and belonging

to the memory of events forming the first epoch of my life—
and a condition of shadow and doubt, appertaining to the pres-
ent, and to the recollection of what constitutes the second
great era of my being. Therefore, what I shall tell of the earlier
period, believe; and to what I may relate of the later time, give
only such credit as may seem due; or doubt it altogether; or,
if doubt it ye cannot, then play unto its riddle the Oedipus.

She whom I loved in youth, and of whom I now pen calmly
and distinctly these remembrances, was the sole daughter of
the only sister of my mother long departed. Eleonora was the
name of my cousin. We had always dwelled together, beneath
a tropical sun, in the Valley of the Many-Colored Grass. No
unguided footstep ever came upon that vale; for it lay far away
up among a range of giant hills that hung beetling around
about it, shutting out the sunlight from its sweetest recesses.
No path was trodden in its vicinity; and, to reach our happy
home, there was need of putting back, with force, the foliage
of many thousands of forest trees, and of crushing to death
the glories of many millions of fragrant flowers. Thus it was
that we lived all alone, knowing nothing of the world without
the valley,—I, and my cousin, and her mother.

From the dim regions beyond the mountains at the upper
end of our encircled domain, there crept out a narrow and
deep river, brighter than all save the eyes of Eleonora; and,
winding stealthily about in mazy courses, it passed away, at
length, through a shadowy gorge, among hills still dimmer
than those whence it had issued. We called it the "River of
Silence:" for there seemed to be a hushing influence in its flow.
No murmur arose from its bed, and so gently it wandered along
that the pearly pebbles upon which we loved to gaze, far down
within its bosom, stirred not at all, but lay in a motionless

content, each in its own old station, shining on gloriously forever.

The margin of the river, and of the many dazzling rivulets that glided, through devious ways, into its channel, as well as the spaces that extended from the margins away down into the depths of the streams until they reached the bed of pebbles at the bottom,—these spots, not less than the whole surface of the valley, from the river to the mountains that girdled it in, were carpeted all by a soft green grass, thick, short, perfectly even, and vanilla-perfumed, but so besprinkled throughout with the yellow buttercup, the white daisy, the purple violet, and the ruby-red asphodel, that its exceeding beauty spoke to our hearts, in loud tones, of the love and of the glory of God.

And, here and there, in groves about this grass, like wildernesses of dreams, sprang up fantastic trees, whose tall slender stems stood not upright, but slanted gracefully toward the light that peered at noon-day into the centre of the valley. Their bark was speckled with the vivid alternate splendor of ebony and silver, and was smoother than all save the cheeks of Eleonora; so that, but for the brilliant green of the huge leaves that spread from their summits in long tremulous lines, dallying with the Zephyrs, one might have fancied them giant serpents of Syria doing homage to their Sovereign the Sun.

Hand in hand about this valley, for fifteen years, roamed I with Eleonora before Love entered within our hearts. It was one evening at the close of the third lustrum of her life, and of the fourth of my own, that we sat, locked in each other's embrace, beneath the serpent-like trees, and looked down within the waters of the River of Silence at our images therein. We spoke no words during the rest of that sweet day; and our words even upon the morrow were tremulous and few. We had drawn the god Eros from that wave, and now felt that he had enkindled within us the fiery souls of our forefathers. The passions which had for centuries distinguished our race came thronging with the fancies for which they had been equally noted, and together breathed a delirious bliss over the Valley of the Many-Colored Grass. A change fell upon all things. Strange brilliant flowers, star-shaped, burst out upon the trees where no flowers had been known before. The tints of the green carpet deepened; and when, one by one, the white daisies shrank away, there sprang up, in place of them, ten by ten of the ruby-red asphodel. And life arose in our paths; for the tall flamingo, hitherto unseen, with all gay glowing birds, flaunted his scarlet plumage before us. The golden and silver fish haunted the river, out of the bosom of which issued, little by little, a murmur that swelled, at length, into a lulling melody more divine than that of the harp of Aeolus—sweeter than all save the voice of Eleonora. And now, too, a voluminous cloud, which we had long watched in the regions of Hesper, floated out thence, all gorgeous in crimson and gold, and settling in peace above us, sank, day by day, lower and lower, until its edges rested upon the tops of the mountains, turning all their dimness into magnificence, and shutting us up, as if forever, within a magic prison-house of grandeur and of glory.

The loveliness of Eleonora was that of the Seraphim; but she was a maiden artless and innocent as the brief life she had led among the flowers. No guile disguised the fervor of love which animated her heart, and she examined with me its inmost recesses as we walked together in the Valley of the Many-Colored Grass, and discoursed of the mighty changes which had lately taken place therein.

At length, having spoken one day, in tears, of the last sad

change which must befall Humanity, she thenceforward dwelt only upon this one sorrowful theme, interweaving it into all our converse, as, in the songs of the bard of Schiraz, the same images are found occurring, again and again, in every impressive variation of phrase.

She had seen that the finger of Death was upon her bosom—that, like the ephemeron, she had been made perfect in loveliness only to die; but the terrors of the grave, to her, lay solely in a consideration which she revealed to me, one evening at twilight, by the banks of the River of Silence. She grieved to think that, having entombed her in the Valley of the Many-Colored Grass, I would quit forever its happy recesses, transferring the love which now was so passionately her own to some maiden of the outer and every-day world. And, then and there, I threw myself hurriedly at the feet of Eleonora, and offered up a vow, to herself and to Heaven, that I would never bind myself in marriage to any daughter of Earth—that I would in no manner prove recreant to her dear memory, or to the memory of the devout affection with which she had blessed me. And I called the Mighty Ruler of the Universe to witness the pious solemnity of my vow. And the curse which I invoked of *Him* and of her, a saint in Helusion, should I prove traitorous to that promise, involved a penalty the exceeding great horror of which will not permit me to make record of it here. And the bright eyes of Eleonora grew brighter at my words; and she sighed as if a deadly burthen had been taken from her breast; and she trembled and very bitterly wept; but she made acceptance of the vow, (for what was she but a child?) and it made easy to her the bed of her death. And she said to me, not many days afterwards, tranquilly dying, that, because of what I had done for the comfort of her spirit, she would watch over me in that spirit when departed, and, if so it were permitted her, return to me visibly in the watches of the night; but, if this thing were, indeed, beyond the power of the souls in Paradise, that she would, at least, give me frequent indications of her presence; sighing upon me in the evening winds, or filling the air which I breathed with perfume from the censers of the angels. And, with these words upon her lips, she yielded up her innocent life, putting an end to the first epoch of my own.

Thus far I have faithfully said. But as I pass the barrier in Time's path formed by the death of my beloved, and proceed with the second era of my existence, I feel that a shadow gathers over my brain, and I mistrust the perfect sanity of the record. But let me on. —Years dragged themselves along heavily, and still I dwelled within the Valley of the Many-Colored Grass;—but a second change had come upon all things. The star-shaped flowers shrank into the stems of the trees, and appeared no more. The tints of the green carpet faded; and, one by one, the ruby-red asphodels withered away; and there sprang up, in place of them, ten by ten, dark eye-like violets that writhed uneasily and were encumbered with dew. And Life departed from our paths; for the tall flamingo flaunted no longer his scarlet plumage before us, but flew sadly from the vale into the hills, with all the gay glowing birds that had arrived in his company. And the golden and silver fish swam down through the gorge at the lower end of our domain and bedecked the sweet river never again. And the lulling melody that had been softer than the wind-harp of Aeolus and more divine than all save the voice of Eleonora, it died little by little away, in murmurs growing lower and lower, until the stream returned, at length, utterly, into the solemnity of its original silence. And then, lastly the voluminous cloud uprose, and, abandoning the tops of the mountains to the dimness of old, fell back into the regions of Hesper, and took away all its manifold golden and gorgeous glories from the Valley of the Many-Colored Grass.

Yet the promises of Eleonora were not forgotten; for I heard the sounds of the swinging of the censers of the angels; and streams of a holy perfume floated ever and ever about the valley; and at lone hours, when my heart beat heavily, the winds that bathed my brow came unto me laden with soft sighs; and indistinct murmurs filled often the night air; and once—oh, but once only! I was awakened from a slumber like the slumber of death by the pressing of spiritual lips upon my own.

But the void within my heart refused, even thus, to be filled. I longed for the love which had before filled it to overflowing. At length the valley *pained* me through its memories of Eleonora, and I left it forever for the vanities and the turbulent triumphs of the world.

I found myself within a strange city, where all things might have served to blot from recollection the sweet dreams I had dreamed so long in the Valley of the Many-Colored Grass. The pomps and pageantries of a stately court, and the mad clangor of arms, and the radiant loveliness of woman, bewildered and intoxicated my brain. But as yet my soul had proved true to its vows, and the indications of the presence of Eleonora were still given me in the silent hours of the night. Suddenly, these manifestations they ceased; and the world grew dark before mine eyes; and I stood aghast at the burning thoughts which possessed—at the terrible temptations which beset me; for there came from some far, far distant and unknown land, into the gay court of the king I served, a maiden to whose beauty my whole recreant heart yielded at once—at whose footstool I bowed down without a struggle, in the most ardent, in the most abject worship of love. What indeed was my passion for the young girl of the valley in comparison with the fervor, and the delirium, and the spirit-lifting ecstasy of adoration with which I poured out my whole soul in tears at the feet of the ethereal Ermengarde?—Oh bright was the seraph Ermengarde! and in that knowledge I had room for none other. —Oh divine was the angel Ermengarde! and as I looked down into the depths of her memorial eyes I thought only of them—and of *her.*

I wedded;—nor dreaded the curse I had invoked; and its bitterness was not visited upon me. And once—but once again in the silence of the night, there came through my lattice the soft sighs which had forsaken me; and they modelled themselves into familiar and sweet voice, saying:

"Sleep in peace!—for the Spirit of Love reigneth and ruleth, and, in taking to thy passionate heart her who is Ermengarde, thou art absolved, for reasons which shall be made known to thee in Heaven, of thy vows unto Eleonora."

AFTERWORD

AT THE END of *Eleonora's* second paragraph, Poe invites the reader to play Oedipus to the riddle of his tale's conclusion, and one pertinently recalls that the riddle of the Sphinx, which Oedipus guessed, had to do with the ages of man's life. *Eleonora* is a first-person account or depiction of four stages in the life of a particular sort of man, a man who was born with an inherited "vigor of fancy" and has developed into a visionary whose dreams explore the "light ineffable" and the *mare tene-brarum* or "sea of darkness." Given such a narrator, we should not look for any mundane realism in his narrative; it is clear from the beginning that we shall not be told what the characters have for dinner, or whether they wear socks and shoes. On the other hand, it would be a pity to mistake this story for the airy fabrications and misrememberings of a madman. *Eleonora's* poet-hero tells his tale, and tells it truly, but as so often in Poe the narrative mode is allegory.

For the gnostic or neo-Platonist, the soul's adventure entails an original unity with God, a descent into incarnate life and the corruption of this world, and a subsequent effort to extricate itself and return to its first condition. Poe's fiction repeatedly employs this story-pattern, in whole or in part; we have it in that focal story *Ligeia,* for example, but there the allegory is ambiguous and dark; the later *Eleonora,* for all its luxury of detail, is perhaps the clearest and most charming embodiment of Poe's essential plot. Like Ligeia, the seraphic Eleonora stands for "the Idea of Beauty," that mediatory principle through which the divine is known to men, and the hero's relation to her, during the first stage of his life, represents the unfallen condition of his soul. That condition is reflected in the original aspect of the Valley, which is Edenically isolated from the "world," which partakes of the eternal (so we feel through the prominence of such words as "always" and "forever,") and which through all of its beauties speaks to the hero "of the love and of the glory of God." The second phase of the hero's life begins when his love of Beauty is tarnished by the activation of his hereditary "ardor of passion." The state of soul which ensues is mirrored in the color, life, and melody of the transformed Valley, which for all its splendor is a garish parody of blessedness and implies a spiritual fall. A prisoner of Eros and of Venus (Hesper), Poe's poet-hero has forsaken "the Beauty above" for a physical passion incompatible with it, and must therefore suffer the loss of his mediatrix. With Eleonora's death, there comes a third period in which the Valley withers and grieves, and the hero's damaged soul is solaced only by his memories of Eleonora, and by her occasional visitations. It will be noted that the Eleonora with whom he now fitfully communes is not an object of passion but the angelic spirit whom first he knew; his grief is thus to be seen as purgative, and a fortifying preparation for the trials of the fourth phase of his life. Leaving the Valley for a city in which he encounters "the vanities and the turbulent triumphs of the world," the hero finds himself subject to every base temptation, and in danger of forgetting his original harmony with God. This is restored through the seeming infidelity of his marriage to Ermengarde—seeming, I say, because it is quite plain that Ermengarde is somehow Eleonora *rediviva*. Both names begin with an E; Ermengarde is not of the city or "world," but comes to it from a "far, far distant and unknown land"—Helusion, or the Valley; like Eleonora she is bright, seraphic, and conducive to worship; she is authenticated by a voice from Heaven; and her "memorial eyes" (like those of Ligeia) can signify only that the hero, through her, is once again able to ignore the world and "remember his Creator." It is fruitless to try to decide by what means—reincarnation, possession, angelic visitation—Eleonora has returned. On the plane of plot the final action is mysterious, but as allegory it is transparent: Eleonora and Ermengarde (on whose likeness the first version of the tale was still more insistent) together constitute the *forma specifica* which guarantees the hero's salvation, and the hero's marriage is allegorically an *anamnesis*, the regaining of a previous state of awareness in which the hero's intact soul participated in supernal harmony and beauty.

Commentators sometimes speak of Poe's "style," as if he had but one way of writing. The fact is that he chose numerous styles for his several modes and purposes, distinguishing between the means appropriate to criticism, fiction, and verse, and attuning the language of his tales to their genres ("grotesque," "arabesque," or other) and the natures of his narrators. Poe's literary theory permitted the prose tale a degree of "truth" or verisimilitude, and a fullness and clarity of plot not appropriate in poetry; at the same time he required that the tale possess, if it hoped for any imaginative effect, a deep "undercurrent" of allegorical meaning. The poem, on the other hand, was to be vague, bewildering, incantatory, and full of "novel combinations" of the beautiful, to the end of inducing in its reader a dizzy foretaste of unimaginable unities belonging to a higher world of the spirit. In the light of these general prescriptions, *Eleonora* is obviously a hybrid performance. It is a prose tale with a simple plot, but it is wholly lacking in quotidian "truth," and its allegorical "undercurrent" is more readily sounded than any other in Poe's fiction, unless it be *William Wilson*'s. Furthermore, the style of the tale patently aims at certain of the effects which Poe deemed proper to poetry. "Mazy," "wandering," "dazzling," "besprinkled," and "interweaving" are words which appear in Poe's text, and which apply not merely to his subject matter but to the "arabesque" manner of its writing: that is to say, the tale imitates in language a decorative style which the *Britannica* describes as "a fantastic or complicated interweaving" of tendrilous, foliate or floral forms, often (as at Pompeii) heterogeneously incorporating "birds and animals, human figures and chimeras." Poe's intricate and profuse sentences mingle the natural with the preternatural—the buttercup and daisy, for instance, with the "writhing" violet and "fantastic" tree—in such a way as to produce those "novel combinations" by which poetry (à la Poe) seeks to estrange us from the known and impel us toward the beyond. Another aspect of Poe's arabesque style is his mingling of rhetorics: there is the plainness of "We will say, then, that I am mad;" there is also such a phrase as "Suddenly, these manifestations they ceased; and the world grew dark before mine eyes," in which we find both a French construction and an archaism; while in the paragraph concerning Eleonora's death there is a cascade of "Biblical" sentences beginning with "And." One is reminded, in experiencing Poe's shifts of style, of the dazzling eclecticism of such arabesque interiors as he describes in *The Assignation* or *Ligeia*.

It need hardly be pointed out that there are further devices, in this prose tale, which are calculated to produce what Poe meant by the poetic effect. The phrase, "brighter than all save the eyes of Eleonora," is repeated with variations, and suggests a verse refrain. The technique of recapitulation, so prominent in late incantatory poems like "Ulalume" and "Annabel Lee," is liberally used, and especially so in the descriptive paragraph which follows Eleonora's death: one might say of this tale, as its narrator says of the poetry of Hafiz, that in it "the same images are found occurring, again and again, in every impressive variation of phrase." Finally, it will be noted that the penultimate paragraph threatens, in its first four words, to break into emphatic meter and rhyme.

Poe's arabesque prose in *Eleonora,* with its strange fusions and its supporting poetic devices, is clearly intended, then, not merely to tell a tale but to excite in the reader "the Poetic Sentiment"; I take this as a further certification that the narrator's concluding visions are not to be discounted as "mad," but accepted and in a measure *shared*. When prose or poetry sets out to enchant and enthrall, and to any extent succeeds, it is possible for the reader to grow passively unaware of particular words and strategies, and I therefore wish to conclude by mentioning a few details of *Eleonora*'s deliberate texture. There is, for one thing, an admirably subtle use of light and dark and shadow throughout the story. The "forever" of the Valley's first state is tellingly altered in the second to "as if forever," and there are many such deft modulations to be found. The narrator's opening words about "the wisdom which is of good" and "the mere knowledge which is of evil" hint at Eden and the Fall, and prepare one to discern foreboding elements in the Valley as first described: the asphodel (which ambiguously symbolizes both death and Elysian immortality) is accordingly not white or yellow but an unnatural "ruby-red," and there are trees which resemble serpents. When the hero succumbs to Eros, it is appropriately "beneath the serpent-like trees," and thereafter the asphodel, unambiguously suggestive of passion and death, crowds out the purity of the white daisies.

More often than is generally appreciated, Poe reinforces his meaning by the artful employment of allusion or echo. It may well be that *Eleonora*'s use of the asphodel is intended, among other things, to evoke the carnal context of *Paradise Lost*, IX, 1040, and that the violets which weep for Eleonora's death recall Laertes' words at Ophelia's graveside (*Hamlet*, V, i, 261 ff.). We may be sure, however, that the phrase "We spoke no words during the rest of that sweet day" is reminiscent of the famous line in *Inferno*, V, where Francesca, having told of her (and Paolo's) fall into carnal sin through the reading of a poem about Lancelot, concludes by saying *quel giorno più non vi leggemmo avante*—"That day we read in it no further." Still more surely, the Valley's "many-colored grass" puts us in mind of Shelley's famous lines

> *Life, like a dome of many-colored glass,*
> *Stains the white radiance of Eternity,*

and sends us back also to the description of Nesace's palace in Poe's own early poem "Al Aaraaf," where a circular diamond window, set into the dome, diffracts the light of God's Truth into the many colors of Beauty. Finally, when Poe's hero bows down at Ermengarde's footstool "in the most abject worship of love," it seems to me that our memory of Psalm 99—"Exalt ye the Lord our God, and worship at his footstool"—confirms our sense of what sort of emissary she is.

In 1966, I wrote a short essay on John Milton's "companion poems" for Oscar Williams's Master Poems of the English Language, *an anthology in which each poem was briefly introduced to the general reader by some critic or poet-critic.*

Milton's "L'Allegro" and "Il Penseroso"

Hence loathed Melancholy
    Of Cerberus *and blackest midnight born,*
In Stygian *Cave forlorn*
    'Mongst horrid shapes, and shrieks, and sights unholy,
Find out some uncouth cell,
    Where brooding darkness spreads his jealous wings,
And the night-Raven sings;
    There under Ebon *shades, and low-brow'd Rocks,*
As ragged as thy Locks,
    In dark Cimmerian *desert ever dwell.*
But come thou Goddess fair and free,
In Heav'n yclep'd Euphrosyne,
And by men, heart-easing Mirth,
Whom lovely Venus *at a birth*
With two sister Graces more
To Ivy-crowned Bacchus *bore;*
Or whether (as some Sager sing)
The frolic Wind that breathes the Spring,
Zephyr *with* Aurora *playing,*
As he met her once a-Maying,

There on Beds of Violets blue,
And fresh-blown Roses washt in dew,
Fill'd her with thee a daughter fair,
So buxom, blithe, and debonair.
Haste thee nymph, and bring with thee
Jest and youthful Jollity,
Quips and Cranks, and wanton Wiles,
Nods, and Becks, and Wreathed Smiles,
Such as hang on Hebe's cheek,
And love to live in dimple sleek;
Sport that wrinkled Care derides,
And Laughter holding both his sides.
Come, and trip it as ye go
On the light fantastic toe,
And in thy right hand lead with thee,
The Mountain Nymph, sweet Liberty;
And if I give thee honour due,
Mirth, admit me of thy crew
To live with her, and live with thee,
In unreproved pleasures free;
To hear the Lark begin his flight,
And singing startle the dull night,
From his watch-tow'r in the skies,
Till the dappled dawn doth rise;
Then to come in spite of sorrow,
And at my window bid good morrow,
Through the Sweet-Briar, or the Vine,
Or the twisted Eglantine;
While the Cock with lively din,
Scatters the rear of darkness thin,
And to the stack, or the Barn door,

Stoutly struts his Dames before;
Oft list'ning how the Hounds and horn
Cheerly rouse the slumb'ring morn,
From the side of some Hoar Hill,
Through the high wood echoing shrill;
Some time walking not unseen
By Hedge-row Elms, on Hillocks green,
Right against the Eastern gate,
Where the great Sun begins his state,
Rob'd in flames, and Amber light,
The clouds in thousand Liveries dight;
While the Plowman near at hand,
Whistles o'er the Furrow'd Land,
And the Milkmaid singeth blithe,
And the Mower whets his scythe,
And every Shepherd tells his tale
Under the Hawthorn in the dale.
Straight mine eye hath caught new pleasures
Whilst the Lantskip round it measures,
Russet Lawns and Fallows Gray,
Where the nibbling flocks do stray;
Mountains on whose barren breast
The labouring clouds do often rest;
Meadows trim with Daisies pied,
Shallow Brooks, and Rivers wide.
Towers and Battlements it sees
Bosom'd high in tufted Trees,
Where perhaps some beauty lies,
The Cynosure of neighbouring eyes.
Hard by, a Cottage chimney smokes,
From betwixt two aged Oaks,

Where Corydon *and* Thyrsis *met,*
Are at their savoury dinner set
Of Herbs, and other Country Messes,
Which the neat-handed Phyllis *dresses;*
And then in haste her Bow'r she leaves,
With Thestylis *to bind the Sheaves;*
Or if the earlier season lead
To the tann'd Haycock in the Mead.
Sometimes with secure delight
The up-land Hamlets will invite,
When the merry Bells ring round,
And the jocund rebecks sound
To many a youth, and many a maid,
Dancing in the Chequer'd shade;
And young and old come forth to play
On a Sunshine Holiday,
Till the live-long day-light fail;
Then to the Spicy Nut-brown Ale,
With stories told of many a feat,
How Faery Mab *the junkets eat;*
She was pincht and pull'd, she said,
And he, by Friar's Lanthorn led,
Tells how the drudging Goblin *sweat*
To earn his Cream-bowl duly set,
When in one night, ere glimpse of morn,
His shadowy Flail hath thresh'd the Corn
That ten day-labourers could not end;
Then lies him down the Lubber Fiend,
And, stretch'd out all the Chimney's length,
Basks at the fire his hairy strength;
And Crop-full out of doors he flings,

Ere the first Cock his Matin rings.
Thus done the Tales, to bed they creep,
By whispering Winds soon lull'd asleep.
Tow'red Cities please us then,
And the busy hum of men,
Where throngs of Knights and Barons bold,
In weeds of Peace high triumphs hold,
With store of Ladies, whose bright eyes
Rain influence, and judge the prize
Of Wit, or Arms, while both contend
To win her Grace, whom all commend.
There let Hymen *oft appear*
In Saffron robe, with Taper clear,
And pomp, and feast, and revelry,
With mask, and antique Pageantry—
Such sights as youthful Poets dream
On Summer eves by haunted stream.
Then to the well-trod stage anon,
If Jonson's *learned Sock be on,*
Or sweetest Shakespeare, *fancy's child,*
Warble his native Wood-notes wild.
And ever against eating Cares,
Lap me in soft Lydian *Airs,*
Married to immortal verse,
Such as the meeting soul may pierce
In notes, with many a winding bout
Of linked sweetness long drawn out,
With wanton heed, and giddy cunning,
The melting voice through mazes running;
Untwisting all the chains that tie
The hidden soul of harmony;

That Orpheus' self may heave his head
From golden slumber on a bed
Of heapt Elysian flow'rs, and hear
Such strains as would have won the ear
Of Pluto, to have quite set free
His half-regain'd Eurydice.
These delights if thou canst give,
Mirth, with thee I mean to live.

IL PENSEROSO

Hence vain deluding joys,
  The brood of folly without father bred,
How little you bested,
  Or fill the fixed mind with all your toys;
Dwell in some idle brain,
  And fancies fond with gaudy shapes possess,
As thick and numberless
  As the gay motes that people the Sun-Beams,
Or likest hovering dreams,
  The fickle Pensioners of Morpheus' train.
But hail thou Goddess, sage and holy,
Hail divinest Melancholy,
Whose Saintly visage is too bright
To hit the Sense of human sight;
And therefore to our weaker view,
O'erlaid with black, staid Wisdom's hue.
Black, but such as in esteem,
Prince Memnon's sister might beseem,
Or that Starr'd Ethiop Queen that strove
To set her beauty's praise above

The Sea Nymphs, and their powers offended.
Yet thou art higher far descended;
Thee bright-hair'd Vesta long of yore,
To solitary Saturn bore;
His daughter she (in Saturn's reign,
Such mixture was not held a stain).
Oft in glimmering Bow'rs and glades
He met her, and in secret shades
Of woody Ida's inmost grove,
While yet there was no fear of Jove.
Come pensive Nun, devout and pure,
Sober, steadfast, and demure,
All in a robe of darkest grain,
Flowing with majestic train,
And sable stole of Cypress Lawn,
Over thy decent shoulders drawn.
Come, but keep thy wonted state,
With ev'n step, and musing gait,
And looks commercing with the skies,
Thy rapt soul sitting in thine eyes:
There held in holy passion still,
Forget thyself to Marble, till
With a sad Leaden downward cast,
Thou fix them on the earth as fast.
And join with thee calm Peace and Quiet,
Spare Fast, that oft with gods doth diet,
And hears the Muses in a ring
Aye round about Jove's Altar sing.
And add to these retired Leisure,
That in trim Gardens takes his pleasure;
But first, and chiefest, with thee bring

Him that yon soars on golden wing,
Guiding the fiery-wheeled throne,
The Cherub Contemplation;
And the mute Silence hist along,
'Less Philomel will deign a Song,
In her sweetest, saddest plight,
Smoothing the rugged brow of night,
While Cynthia checks her Dragon yoke,
Gently o'er th' accustom'd Oak;
Sweet Bird that shunn'st the noise of folly,
Most musical, most melancholy!
Thee Chantress oft the Woods among,
I woo to hear thy even-Song;
And missing thee, I walk unseen
On the dry smooth-shaven Green,
To behold the wand'ring Moon,
Riding near her highest noon,
Like one that had been led astray
Through the Heav'n's wide pathless way;
And oft, as if her head she bow'd,
Stooping through a fleecy cloud.
Oft on a Plat of rising ground,
I hear the far-off Curfew sound,
Over some wide-water'd shore,
Swinging slow with sullen roar;
Or if the Air will not permit,
Some still removed place will fit,
Where glowing Embers through the room
Teach light to counterfeit a gloom,
Far from all resort of mirth,
Save the Cricket on the hearth,

Or the Bellman's drowsy charm,
To bless the doors from nightly harm:
Or let my Lamp at midnight hour,
Be seen in some high lonely Tow'r,
Where I may oft out-watch the Bear,
With thrice great Hermes, *or unsphere*
The spirit of Plato *to unfold*
What Worlds, or what vast Regions hold
The immortal mind that hath forsook
Her mansion in this fleshly nook:
And of those Dæmons *that are found*
In fire, air, flood, or under ground,
Whose power hath a true consent
With Planet, or with Element.
Sometime let Gorgeous Tragedy
In Scepter'd Pall come sweeping by,
Presenting Thebes, *or* Pelops' *line,*
Or the tale of Troy *divine,*
Or what (though rare) of later age,
Ennobled hath the Buskin'd stage.
But, O sad Virgin, that thy power
Might raise Musaeus *from his bower,*
Or bid the soul of Orpheus *sing*
Such notes as, warbled to the string,
Drew iron tears down Pluto's *cheek,*
And made Hell grant what Love did seek.
Or call up him that left half told
The story of Cambuscan *bold,*
Of Camball, *and of* Algarsife,
And who had Canace *to wife,*
That own'd the virtuous Ring and Glass,

And of the wond'rous Horse of Brass,
On which the Tartar King did ride;
And if aught else great Bards beside
In sage and solemn tunes have sung,
Of Tourneys and of Trophies hung,
Of Forests, and inchantments drear,
Where more is meant than meets the ear.
Thus night oft see me in thy pale career,
Till civil-suited Morn appear,
Not trickt and frounc't as she was wont
With the Attic Boy to hunt,
But Kerchieft in a comely Cloud,
While rocking Winds are Piping loud,
Or usher'd with a shower still,
When the gust hath blown his fill,
Ending on the rustling Leaves,
With minute drops from off the Eaves.
And when the Sun begins to fling
His flaring beams, me Goddess bring
To arched walks of twilight groves,
And shadows brown that Sylvan loves
Of Pine or monumental Oak,
Where the rude Axe with heaved stroke
Was never heard the Nymphs to daunt,
Or fright them from their hallow'd haunt.
There in close covert by some Brook,
Where no profaner eye may look,
Hide me from Day's garish eye,
While the Bee with Honied thigh,
That at her flow'ry work doth sing,
And the Waters murmuring

With such consort as they keep,
Entice the dewy-feather'd Sleep;
And let some strange mysterious dream
Wave at his Wings in Airy stream,
Of lively portraiture display'd,
Softly on my eye-lids laid.
And as I wake, sweet music breathe
Above, about, or underneath,
Sent by some spirit to mortals good,
Or th'unseen Genius of the Wood.
But let my due feet never fail
To walk the studious Cloister's pale,
And love the high embowed Roof,
With antic Pillars massy proof,
And storied Windows richly dight,
Casting a dim religious light.
There let the pealing Organ blow
To the full voic'd Quire below,
In Service high and Anthems clear,
As may with sweetness, through mine ear,
Dissolve me into extasies,
And bring all Heav'n before mine eyes.
And may at last my weary age
Find out the peaceful hermitage,
The Hairy Gown and Mossy Cell,
Where I may sit and rightly spell
Of every Star that Heav'n doth shew,
And every Herb that sips the dew;
Till old experience do attain
To something like Prophetic strain.
These pleasures Melancholy give,
And I with thee will choose to live.

THESE COMPANION POEMS have been much and well dis-
cussed, but until such recent studies as D. C. Allen's they have
generally been denied any complexity or weight. It is not hard
to see why that has happened. "L'Allegro" and "Il Penseroso"
do not have such conspicuous verbal wit as characterizes some
other works of Milton's youth; elegant logic, bold word play,
and virtuoso similes are lacking, and therefore it has been easy
to take the poems for simple and charming exercises. They have
been thought to consist mainly of brief, pleasant and general-
ized evocations of the preferred experiences of the Cheerful or
Enjoying Man, on the one hand, and the Thoughtful Man on
the other.

But these are witty poems; and their wit, which is the index
of their seriousness, must initially be found in the implications
of their structure. One may see at first glance that the two po-
ems develop in a similar manner: "L'Allegro" begins with a dis-
missal of Melancholy and then, having summoned Mirth and
Liberty and their train, proceeds to consider the ways in which
a cheerful man might divert himself from dawn until late at
night; "Il Penseroso" begins with a dismissal of "vain, deluding
joys" and then, having summoned Melancholy, Contemplation,
and their train, proceeds to consider what might—between eve-
ning and morning—content the thoughtful man. Perceiving
such broad resemblances in structure, the reader will perhaps
feel challenged to decide what these poems are to each other:
are they to be contrasted in their subjects, or compared, or
treated as complementary, or seen as indifferently parallel?

An initial clue is to be found in the fact that the Melancholy
dismissed at the opening of "L'Allegro" is not the serenely pon-
dering kind described in the neighboring poem, but a condition
of social and mental alienation; moreover, the redundancy of
the passage, which in ten lines offers us *blackest, Stygian,*

darkness, Raven, Ebon, and *dark,* implies a tone of deadpan jocularity. The corresponding lines of "Il Penseroso," though suitably less extravagant, resemble the dismissal passage of "L'Allegro" in that they are directed not against the moderate enjoyments of Milton's cheerful man, but against empty foolishness. The poems, in short, pretend to attack each other but do not, and their initial relationship is one of sham debate. The implication of this might be that *allegro* and *penseroso* are not mutually exclusive, not necessarily at war, and may in fact be the comfortably alternating moods of a single personality.

This last possibility is strengthened by Milton's refusal, in the invocation of "L'Allegro," to settle for the traditional parentage of Euphrosyne. Bacchus and Venus would beget a sensual and appetitive Mirth, and Milton is not after that sort of cheerfulness; he therefore contrives a sager myth of his own, in which Euphrosyne is begotten by Zephyr (the West Wind) and Aurora (the Dawn) on the freshest of spring mornings. The resultant goddess, who will preside over the pleasures of the first poem, is a chaste and delicate spirit, not deeply incompatible with her rival Melancholy, whose descent from Saturn and Vesta argues purity and contemplative solitude. Judging by their invocations, then, the companion poems celebrate two dispositions that, whatever their differences, agree in respect of chastity, and indicate, by their exclusion of sensuality, that they belong not to men generally but to a particular kind of man.

As the two poems proceed to catalogue the gratifications of the cheerful man and the thoughtful man, the impression that these are alternative aspects of one personality is continually strengthened. Both men are walkers; both have literary sensibilities; both are fond of the drama, and of music, and make reference to Orpheus. Less obviously, and more importantly, the two are approached to one another by their common qualities of detachment, leisureliness, and freedom from "care." The cheerful man is at no time imagined as a participant in anything; he enjoys all serenely at a distance, as spectator or auditor, and the closest he comes to gregariousness is in his willingness to be "not unseen" in his country rambles, or to join the (unmentioned) audience of a comedy or concert. Nor does the cheerful man's world oppose itself by garish brightness to the dim milieux of the other poem; "L'Allegro's" morning sun may be "rob'd in flames," but for the most part the poem's shade and quiet color suggest no quarrel with "Il Penseroso," but a measure of affinity.

There are also, needless to say, salient differences between the two poems, which the similarities serve to emphasize: the towers and stars of one poem are significantly *not* the towers and stars of the other, and so on. But these differences are more readily understood once one has arrived—prompted again by the structure—at the logic of each poem's list of pleasures. "L'Allegro's" list, because it begins at daybreak and proceeds horologically, may seem at first to represent "a day in the life of a cheerful man," but one soon apprehends (through its hesitation between possibilities) that it is really a series of tentative envisionings by such a man, in which he considers what—depending on the hour and the season—it would "oft" or "some time" suit him to see or hear. The enumeration of pleasures progresses from dawn until some indefinite hour of the night, but this is not its only progression: we move also from country peasants and their frolics to city aristocrats and sophisticated entertainments; from naive and everyday sense-experience to refined and exquisite sense-experience. The details of this development cannot be traced here, but the idea, once grasped, is easily applied. It is easy to see how, beginning with perceptions or visions of plants, animals, and rustics, the cheerful man contemplates a sensuous world progressively transformed and spiritualized by fancy, by convention, by manners, by ceremony, and by art. The poem climbs a ladder of aesthetic experience, which begins with bird song and ends with the ecstatic intricacies of Lydian music. What is implied, as we soon come to see, is a way of life: the way of life of an aesthete or artist, whose whole activity is the distillation of beauty from the raw materials of everyday existence.

If we now turn to "Il Penseroso," and to the characterization of Melancholy, we are at once aware of a decided contrast. Whereas Mirth was a spirit devoted to sense data, to enjoyable perceptions of the eye and ear, Melancholy is clothed in an invisible, transcendental light, and is associated from the first with the supersensuous. As a child of the Golden Age, when heaven and earth were at one, she sponsors a kind of contemplation that continually refers what is "below" to what is "above," and seeks to redeem and transmute the leaden actualities of our fallen world. The thoughtful man's pleasures, like those of his alter ego, are presented in an ascending scale of value. First comes the sort of sense experience that might suit his solitary mood, and prompt his kind of spiritual musing: the nightingale puts him in mind of a chantress at vespers, and the watchman seems to intone a blessing. Second, we have his pursuit, through science, philosophy, or art, of the hidden truths of this world and the next; third, his arrival by way of such knowledge at an intimate communion with divine harmonies in nature; and finally, his attainment through worship to ecstatic glimpses of heaven. The reader should notice how the account of the morning, and of the morning walk, is full of words—beginning with *Kerchieft, Piping, usher'd,* and *arched*—that remind one of a church service, the effect being that the natural world, thus suggestively "hallowed," becomes a figurative narthex to the literal church which follows. As this example shows, Milton's twin poems do, after all, contain verbal wit; but the wordplay does not really stand forth, or disclose its serious drift, until the reader has begun to make out the intention of the structure.

"Il Penseroso" closes with the hope that "old experience" will "attain/ To something like Prophetic strain," and this may persuade the reader that the companion poems are sequentially related—that they propose a kind of ideal biography, in which a sensitive, temperate man devotes his youth to aesthetic pleasure, and his riper years to the still higher joys of philosophy and religion. This is certainly a part of the truth: "L'Allegro" does indeed stress youth, and "Il Penseroso" age; taken as a sequence, the poems call for the refinement and final transcendence of sense experience, and the progressive liberation of the soul through a hierarchy of disciplines. But, of course, the relationship of the poems is not merely sequential, it is also rotary: the close of "Il Penseroso" leads back to the opening of "L'Allegro," where "peaceful hermitage" and "Mossy Cell" ("Il Penseroso," lines 168–69) are dismissed as "Stygian" and "uncouth." The implication of this perpetual *da capo* is that the single speaker of these companion poems hopes to alternate, throughout his life's pilgrimage, between the complementary moods and pleasures that they represent—that at any stage of life he will wish himself both *allegro* and *penseroso,* in seasonable proportions. The reading of Plato must not wait, after all, for middle age; a sunshine holiday is, Milton declares, for young and old alike; a life should have aspiring direction, but also a humane fullness and variety.

Like "Lycidas," which finds a Christian consolation within

a pastoral elegy, the companion poems exceed the promise of their convention, although they do so more covertly. These delightful poems, with their short measures and prompt rhymes, may seem at first to do no more than define two dispositions and catalogue their ideal pursuits. Yet as one answers the questions that their structure proposes, one discovers a program for the encompassing of a range of experience, the precise evaluation of its diverse pleasures, and its gradual transmutation toward the knowledge and praise of God. This short essay can offer only a most general statement of Milton's implicit thought; as for the particular relationships within and between the poems, which are of an inexhaustible intricacy and relevance, I leave their study to the fortunate reader. He will find evidence that John Milton was from the beginning, in large patterns and in least details, a master of significant structure and the greatest verse architect in our literature.

In 1985, Stephen Berg invited thirty-one poets, myself
included, to contribute to Singular Voices, a collection
of "new poems with self-interpretive essays."

Some Notes on "Lying"

LYING

To claim, at a dead party, to have spotted a grackle,
When in fact you haven't of late, can do no harm.
Your reputation for saying things of interest
Will not be marred, if you hasten to other topics,
Nor will the delicate web of human trust
Be ruptured by that airy fabrication.
Later, however, talking with toxic zest
Of golf, or taxes, or the rest of it
Where the beaked ladle plies the chuckling ice,
You may enjoy a chill of severance, hearing
Above your head the shrug of unreal wings.
Not that the world is tiresome in itself:
We know what boredom is: it is a dull
Impatience or a fierce velleity,
A champing wish, stalled by our lassitude,
To make or do. In the strict sense, of course,
We invent nothing, merely bearing witness
To what each morning brings again to light:
Gold crosses, cornices, astonishment
Of panes, the turbine-vent which natural law
Spins on the grill-end of the diner's roof,
Then grass and grackles or, at the end of town
In sheen-swept pastureland, the horse's neck

Clothed with its usual thunder, and the stones
Beginning now to tug their shadows in
And track the air with glitter. All these things
Are there before us; there before we look
Or fail to look; there to be seen or not
By us, as by the bee's twelve thousand eyes,
According to our means and purposes.
So too with strangeness not to be ignored,
Total eclipse or snow upon the rose,
And so with that most rare conception, nothing.
What is it, after all, but something missed?
It is the water of a dried-up well
Gone to assail the cliffs of Labrador.
There is what galled the arch-negator, sprung
From Hell to probe with intellectual sight
The cells and heavens of a given world
Which he could take but as another prison:
Small wonder that, pretending not to be,
He drifted through the bar-like boles of Eden
In a black mist low creeping, dragging down
And darkening with moody self-absorption
What, when he left it, lifted and, if seen
From the sun's vantage, seethed with vaulting hues.
Closer to making than the deftest fraud
Is seeing how the catbird's tail was made
To counterpoise, on the mock-orange spray,
Its light, up-tilted spine; or, lighter still,
How the shucked tunic of an onion, brushed
To one side on a backlit chopping-board
And rocked by trifling currents, prints and prints
Its bright, ribbed shadow like a flapping sail.

Odd that a thing is most itself when likened:
The eye mists over, basil hints of clove,
The river glazes toward the dam and spills
To the drubbed rocks below its crashing cullet,
And in the barnyard near the sawdust-pile
Some great thing is tormented. Either it is
A tarp torn loose and in the groaning wind
Now puffed, now flattened, or a hip-shot beast
Which tries again, and once again, to rise.
What, though for pain there is no other word,
Finds pleasure in the cruellest simile?
It is something in us like the catbird's song
From neighbor bushes in the grey of morning
That, harsh or sweet, and of its own accord,
Proclaims its many kin. It is a chant
Of the first springs, and it is tributary
To the great lies told with the eyes half-shut
That have the truth in view: the tale of Chiron
Who, with sage head, wild heart, and planted hoof
Instructed brute Achilles in the lyre,
Or of the garden where we first mislaid
Simplicity of wish and will, forgetting
Out of what cognate splendor all things came
To take their scattering names; and nonetheless
That matter of a baggage-train surprised
By a few Gascons in the Pyrenees—
Which, having worked three centuries and more
In the dark caves of France, poured out at last
The blood of Roland, who to Charles his king
And to the dove that hatched the dovetailed world
Was faithful unto death, and shamed the Devil.

I

Back in the late 1940's, just after World War II, one of my closest Cambridge friends was André du Bouchet, who had come to America as a refugee, studied at Amherst and Harvard, and would soon go back to France to become one of its leading poets. Then, as young men in our twenties, we were quite besotted with poetry, writing it constantly, continually theorizing about it, and translating each other's work. Oddly enough, though we were both earnestly engaged in leftist politics, we were attracted in theory (for a time at least) toward a poetry which should be pure, disrelated, autotelic. André introduced me to Villiers de l'Isle-Adam ("Vivre? Nos valets le feront pour nous"), and I made a translation of Villiers's *Claire Lenoir*. And then there was the example of Raymond Roussel's *Impressions d'Afrique*, which (as I remember) based its fictions upon meaningless puns such as *vers/vers*, and thus achieved a near-perfect impertinence to the world. On one occasion André observed that it would be a pure creative act to announce that one had seen a squirrel in front of the Fogg Museum, if one had *not* seen a squirrel there; one would thus harmlessly and disinterestedly introduce into the minds of one's friends a squirrel which had never existed.

Not long ago, I was fascinated to find, in a memoir of Dylan Thomas by one of his boyhood friends, that the young Thomas had entertained a similar notion. It seemed to him a poetic act to inform his mother that he was carrying a handkerchief in his right-hand pocket, whereas in fact the handkerchief was in his *left*-hand pocket.

My poem "Lying" is not an indictment of du Bouchet and Thomas, whose early aesthetic ideas, like mine, could be briefly, airily, and somewhat jocularly held. But I do owe to them my unreal grackle. It occurred to me (apparently) that a poem about truth and poetry might well start obliquely with a piddling and ludicrous instance of fraudulent "creation," and then proceed to take its implications seriously. It is a fundamental impulse of poetry to refresh the aspect of things. The Dada movement was a mockery and subversion of certain worn-out attitudes toward reality; the unreal-grackle theory of poetry partakes of the same impatience with stale formulations, but it is more extreme and it threatens to touch the thought of even the soberest poet. Because poetry can so charge and heighten the world in language; because it can approach sheer incantation, as in "Pale, beyond porch and portal"; because it can say things like "A deed without a name"; because, when it speaks of "the barren Plains/ Of *Sericana,* where *Chineses* drive/ With Sails and Wind thir cany Waggons light," we are given at least as much magic as information, the poet is prone to the illusion that he can make or unmake the world, or create an alternative reality. This he cannot do, and in proportion as he is touched by that illusion he confesses a timidity about doing what he *can* do— interact with the given world, see and feel and order it newly. W. J. Turner begins a wild and remarkable poem with the line "In despair at being unable to rival the creations of God." It is perhaps because everybody is something of a poet, and can understand that line, that I addressed my poem to "You."

I I

I think I knew from the beginning that Milton's Satan would get into my poem, because the illusory aesthetic of which I've been speaking is ultimately Satanic. Satan, in his insanity, sets himself up as a rival to the Creator, but he can make nothing, and is capable at most of parodies, impostures, and temporary destructions. Did I choose blank verse because I glimpsed Milton in the offing? I suspect that I was more influenced by the fact that pentameter is the most flexible of our meters, and the best in which to build large verse-masses; I must have sensed that, though the drift of the poem would finally be simple, I would wish to deal fluently and amply with the sensible richness of things, and with the world as a dense tissue of resemblances.

The poem assumes that the essential poetic act is the discovery of resemblance, the making of metaphor, and that, the world being one thing, all metaphor tends toward the truth.

III

"Lying," because it is urging the unity of things, expresses the idea not only by near comparisons and far linkages, but also by a certain velocity—by quick shifts and transitions. Does that make sense? I know, for example, that "and nonetheless," in the eighth line from the end, is very sudden and condensed. I leave it to the reader to decide whether all my rapid jumps and splices help to enforce the meaning or not.

What I'm sure of is that a high subject, unless perhaps one is writing a hymn, should not be approached with remorseless nobility, and this poem has its comic elements, as many of mine do. Comedy is serious; it is the voice of balance; and its presence in a serious poem is a test and earnest of its earnestness. One wants anything of moment to be said by the whole self in all its languages. Thus one also includes everyday locutions

("What is it, after all . . ."), ordinary words like "shucked," ordinary things like chopped onions.

I V

More than one reader has said to me that the phrase "Some great thing is tormented" is crucial to the poem, and I agree. The argument had to embrace not only "nature" but also turbine-vents and tarps. It also had to acknowledge suffering as part of the fabric of life, as it does by seeing or imagining a big Holstein with a hopelessly dislocated hip. The catbird, who sings of the kinship of things, sings even of this, though harshly, because the kinship outweighs the suffering. So say I, at any rate.

V

When I first showed "Lying" to my wife, who is always the first and best reader of my poems, she said, "Well, you've finally done it; you've managed to write a poem that's incomprehensible from beginning to end." Then, reading it again, she came to find it, considered as a statement, quite forthright. It seems that "Lying" is the sort of poem which ought first to be heard or read without any distracting anxiety to catch all of its connections and local effects, and that it then asks to be absorbed in several readings or hearings. I make no apology for that: some of the poetry written these days has the relaxed transparency of talk, and would not profit by being mulled over, but much is of the concentrated kind which closes with an implicit *da capo*. Provided it's any good, a poem which took months to write deserves an ungrudging quarter hour from the reader.

I find, in making these notes, that I'm reluctant to expound the obvious, saying for instance that there are "lies" or fictions which are ways of telling the truth, and that the poem ends with three fictions having one burden. What I would most respond to, in conversation with an interested reader, would be noticings or questionings of details: the use of birds throughout, and of the word "shrug" for the hovering of an unreal grackle; the echo of Job, and its intended evocation of a whole passage; the water-figure, strange but not untrue, in which the idea of "nothing" is dismissed; the transformation of the *black mist* into a rainbow; the perching of the catbird on a mock-orange spray; the vitrification of a river, beginning with "glazes" and ending with "cullet." But the fact is that the details are too many for me to worry them in this space; what we have here, I figure, is a baroque poem, in the sense that it is a busy and intricate contraption which issues in plainness.

The following was contributed to David Lehman's
Ecstatic Occasions, Expedient Forms, *a 1987 book in*
which sixty-five poets each chose one of their poems and
told how it had taken shape.

Regarding "Thyme Flowering among Rocks"

This, if Japanese,
Would represent grey boulders
Walloped by rough seas

So that, here or there,
The balked water tossed its froth
Straight into the air.

Here, where things are what
They are, it is thyme blooming,
Rocks, and nothing but—

Having, nonetheless,
Many small leaves implicit,
A green countlessness.

Crouching down, peering
Into perplexed recesses,
You find a clearing

Occupied by sun
Where, along prone, rachitic
Branches, one by one,

Pale stems arise, squared
In the manner of Mentha,
The oblong leaves paired.

One branch, in ending,
Lifts a little and begets
A straight-ascending

Spike, whorled with fine blue
Or purple trumpets, banked in
The leaf-axils. You

Are lost now in dense
Fact, fact which one might have thought
Hidden from the sense,

Blinking at detail
Peppery as this fragrance,
Lost to proper scale

As, in the motion
Of striped fins, a bathysphere
Forgets the ocean.

It makes the craned head
Spin. Unfathomed thyme! The world's
A dream, Basho said,

Not because that dream's
A falsehood, but because it's
Truer than it seems.

BECAUSE I have sent off the worksheets of "Thyme Flowering among Rocks" to a library, I am reduced to making confident guesses as to how its form came about. One thing I know is that I have never deliberately set about to "write heroic couplets" or "write a sonnet." Poetry is both art and craft, but I abominate formal exercises and am stuck with the Emersonian feeling that a poem is something which finds out what it has to say, and in the process discovers the form which will best stress its tone and meaning. It may seem improbable to some poets of the last thirty years that such a process could result in, let us say, a rondeau; but that is because such poets are free-verse practitioners who lack my generation's instinctive sense—got both by reading and by writing—of the capabilities of certain traditional forms.

Though I commonly work in meters, my way of going about a poem is very like the free-verse writer's: that is, I begin by letting the words find what line lengths seem right to them. Often this will result in a stanza of some sort, which (though the ensuing stanzas keep the metrical pattern) will still be flexible enough to permit the argument to move and speak as it likes. All of my poems, therefore, are formally *ad hoc*; quite a few are, so far as I know, without formal precedent, and none sets out to fulfill the "rules" of some standard form. However, I have wakened in the middle of the night to realize that a poem already under way called for the logic of the rondeau; and another poem (I have read my Villon, and translated some of him) told me rather early in the game that it wanted to be a ballade.

The present poem happened because my herb patch reminded me of the miniature landscapes of Japanese gardens, and because grovelling amongst herbs reminded me how much we lose of the world's wonder by perceiving things in an upright posture from usual distances. I expect that the brief way the first lines fell had much to do with expressing minuteness and a moment-by-moment concentrated observation; and that they then, together with the word "Japanese," gave me the notion of using the haiku form as a stanza. I was familiar with the form through such poets as Edmund Blunden, and through Harold G. Henderson's book on the subject. It seems to me that the haiku is the only syllabic form in which the Anglo-American ear can hear quantity with some assurance. Still, because the Japanese register syllables more readily than we, many English haiku rhyme the first and third lines for the sake of greater definition. I chose to rhyme in that manner (or found myself doing it) both for the reason given, and because I was going to write a poem of many haiku, in which variation of rhythm and likely linkages between stanzas would make the haiku pattern less consistently audible. There are poems like Auden's marvelous "In Praise of Limestone" in which we simply do not hear the syllabic structure—the lines in that poem being, if I remember rightly, as long as eleven and fourteen syllables. This inaudibility is not a defect, since the poet was after resistance and self-discipline rather than a clear quantitative effect. What I hope to have got in my little experiment is a quantitative structure of which the reader will be aware, playing against a speech rhythm which carries the motion and emotion.

In Alberta T. Turner's 45 Contemporary Poems *(1985),*
the poets represented were asked to respond to questions
posed by the editor.

About "Cottage Street, 1953"

Framed in her phoenix fire-screen, Edna Ward
Bends to the tray of Canton, pouring tea
For frightened Mrs. Plath; then, turning toward
The pale, slumped daughter, and my wife, and me,

Asks if we would prefer it weak or strong.
Will we have milk or lemon, she enquires?
The visit seems already strained and long.
Each in his turn, we tell her our desires.

It is my office to exemplify
The published poet in his happiness,
Thus cheering Sylvia, who has wished to die;
But half-ashamed, and impotent to bless,

I am a stupid life-guard who has found,
Swept to his shallows by the tide, a girl
Who, far from shore, has been immensely drowned,
And stares through water now with eyes of pearl.

How large is her refusal; and how slight
The genteel chat whereby we recommend
Life, of a summer afternoon, despite
The brewing dusk which hints that it may end.

And Edna Ward shall die in fifteen years,
After her eight-and-eighty summers of

Such grace and courage as permit no tears,
The thin hand reaching out, the last word love,

Outliving Sylvia who, condemned to live,
Shall study for a decade, as she must,
To state at last her brilliant negative
In poems free and helpless and unjust.

1. *Is this poem the record of an actual visit with the Plaths and Edna Ward? Did you know Sylvia only by means of this meeting? How long after the event did you write the poem? Had Sylvia and her work become a "cult" by the time you wrote it?*

In my book *The Mind-Reader*, I offered this little note on the poem: "Edna Ward was Mrs. Herbert D. Ward, my wife's mother. The poet Sylvia Plath (1932–1963) was the daughter of one of Mrs. Ward's Wellesley friends. The recollection is probably composite, but it is true in essentials." I keep no diary, and have a rotten memory, but would swear to this in court: that Mrs. Ward did telephone us in 1953, when we were living nearby in Lincoln, asking us to tea with Mrs. Plath and with her troubled and talented daughter. My wife and I were expected to be sympathetic and encouraging presences, and presumably we accepted the assignment, though our teas with Mrs. Ward and her guests were so many that specific memories elude us. In my mind's eye there is a clear image of the undergraduate Sylvia, "pale, slumped," fearfully withdrawn, and looking, as I later wrote in my notebook, like a *gisant* on a cathedral tomb. That image could have two possible sources: either it derives from Mrs. Ward's tea, or it comes from another occasion on which Sylvia Plath interviewed me for *Mademoiselle*. I met her once again, after her marriage to Ted Hughes, at the house of John Holmes, and found her animated and engaging.

The poem was written in the seventies, when Sylvia (as I shall call her, despite our slight acquaintance) had been established in the canon, and the "confessional" in poetry was an issue. My poem, however, was not conceived as a comment on her reputation or as a consideration, by way of her, of the confessional mode in general.

2. *Could the last line be read as reproof, not only of Sylvia and the excesses of her followers, but of all the self-indulgences of the romantics? Those who are* helpless *cannot be* free; unjust *can mean not only unfair but deformed, untrue, not plumb. Am I overreading?*

The last lines are not intended as reproof. The constellation *brilliant-free-helpless-unjust* is an effort to be fair and downright. The poems of Sylvia's last days were brilliant, and they were free in the sense that they came fast and well; they were helpless and unjust because she was writing out of an ill condition of mind in which she could not do justice to anything but her own feelings. There is a limit to the utility of a poetry so skewed and so personal, but I say that with regret and in no spirit of blame.

"Cottage Street" is sympathetic to Sylvia throughout. It does, however, potentially quarrel with those who glamorize emotional illness and regard suicide as honorific.

3. *Though the poem seems ostensibly to be about Sylvia and about poetry, it also raises such questions as, what is genius for? Is it a tool for fashioning civilization or a means of escape? Is it better to be immensely drowned or a life-guard in the shallows? Is it better to be an Edna Ward, making living your work of art? Do you wish the reader to resolve the questions you raise or to keep asking them?*

The poem does indeed raise such questions. Discussing

them apart from the poem, I'd take the general position that
life is more important than art (though in the greater sense of
art the two are not separable), and that usable orderings of the
world are more valuable than eccentric subjective intensities.
Within the poem, these questions are so weighted, I trust, as
not to make a case against Sylvia; I should like them to add up
to a feeling of regret that a remarkable talent could not have
survived to embrace more of common experience. It is not se-
riously assumed that poetry unlike Sylvia's must be shallow.

4. *The form of the poem exemplifies the restrained, balanced,
gracious Edna Ward point of view, the acceptance and shaping
of existence rather than a brilliant refusal. The stanzas are com-
plete thoughts, the meter regular, the rhymes exact, the syntax
and diction formal. Yet in them the winds of disorder churn:
"frightened Mrs. Plath," "pale, slumped daughter," the strained
atmosphere, the shame and impotence of the published poet, the
possible choices between milk and lemon, weak and strong tea,
life and death, and the shallows of the life-guard compared to the
immensities of Sylvia's sea. To what extent did you consciously
select and shape the poem's form to emphasize this irony in the
situation?*

The pentameter quatrain is a familiar form in which definite
rhythmic meanings may be conveyed to people who still have
the hang of reading metrical verse. For example, the second
quatrain of "Cottage Street" contains four end-stopped lines of
no great rhythmic élan, which together with such subverted
words as "strong" and "desires" give a sense of confinement,
tedium, and tepidity. All of this contrasts with the free move-
ment and wrenched, complex grammar of lines 12–16, which
speak of Sylvia's having been "immensely drowned." I believe
that this contrast of movement (and of words) may operate in

three ways. First, it sets the intensity of Sylvia's suffering against a background which is low keyed and comfortably routine. Second, it may imply the nullity of the everyday as perceived by someone painfully self-absorbed. Third, it prepares, as "slight" and "genteel chat" continue to prepare, for a species of counter-statement in stanza six. I am better acquainted with depression and alienation than some who romanticize them, and I know that mental anguish can be "immense"; but there is also magnitude in a long life well lived in the world of others, and stanza six, without chiding Sylvia, laments that she was deprived of those dimensions. For those with whom the poem potentially quarrels, stanza six amounts to a reminder that the world is dull only to the dull or ill, and that mental illness entails a shrinkage of awareness and sensibility.

5. *How was the poem started? What changes did you make and in what order? Would you change the poem in any way if you were doing it now? If you have saved the worksheets, could I see copies of them?*

I daresay that the poem was written, as is usual with me, very slowly from beginning to end, with much tinkering in the process but no revision thereafter. At some time not long after Edna Ward's death, I wrote a few words in my notebook amounting to a suggestion that I might be able to make, out of my sketchy memories of a tea in Wellesley, a poem which would, in a short space, and with some atmospheric and emotional force, say all the things mentioned in 2, 3, and 4 above. I imagine that I got 'round to writing the poem when a good first line occurred to me.

6. *What other questions would you have liked me to ask?*

You might have asked, in view of my testimony, whether my poem has generally been taken as I meant it. I recall that one malign reviewer, perhaps in *The New Republic,* took it for an attack on Sylvia, and that two young women, fresh from some course in "American Women's Poetry from Phyllis Wheatley to the Present," once came to me for reassurances. But on the whole, those who have testified about "Cottage Street" seem to have understood what sort of balancing act I intended. I am glad of that, because I feel that a poem which doesn't largely control the responses of a trained reader has not done the job.

Movies and Dreams

I

These comments about poetry and film were written for Man and The Movies *(1967), which was edited by W. R. Robinson.*

IT IS HARD to say offhand how much one's art may have been tinctured by one's seeing of motion pictures, because watching film is (for me, for most) so much less judicial and analytic than other art experience. The conventions are transparent, the molding of the imagination is insidious. Even the worst movie has much of the authority of the actual, and quite without knowing it one comes out of the theater brainwashed into scanning the world through the norms of the camera. The enthusiasts of the pittoresco at the close of the eighteenth century, rapturously arranging the landscape in their Claude glasses, were conscious of the imposition; the moviegoer walks about taking shots and sequences unaware. The same entrancement characterizes the moviegoer's acquisition of personal style; to put on an Old Vic accent, to ape the gestures of a stage actor or actress—these involve some deliberate imposture, but to smoke like George Raft, to lift the eyebrows like Cary Grant— that is another and more hypnotized order of imitation. The mannerisms of movie stars, unconsciously borrowed and recognized without specific reminiscence, have for us something of the universality of the Italian vocabulary of gestures, though of course they are more transitory.

Knowing how far my mind's eye must have been conditioned by motion pictures, I venture with diffidence the opinion that certain pre-Edison poetry was genuinely cinematic. Whenever, for example, I read *Paradise Lost*, I, 44–58 (the long shot of Satan's fall from Heaven to Hell, the panorama of the rebels rolling in the lake of fire, the sudden close-up of Satan's afflicted eyes), I feel that I am experiencing a passage which, though its effects may have been suggested by the spatial surprises of Baroque architecture, is facilitated for me, and not misleadingly, by my familiarity with screen techniques. If this reaction is not anachronistic foolishness, it follows that one must be wary in attributing this or that aspect of any contemporary work to the influence of film.

But glancing at my own poems, as the editor has invited me to do, I find in a number of pieces—"Marginalia" for instance —what may owe as much to the camera as to the sharp noticing of poets like Hopkins and Ponge: a close and rapid scanning of details, an insubordination of authenticating particulars, abrupt shifting in lieu of the full-dress rhetorical transition. Here is a bit of the poem mentioned:

> *Things concentrate at the edges; the pond-surface*
> *Is bourne to fish and man and it is spread*
> *In textile scum and damask light, on which*
> *The lily-pads are set; and there are also*
> > *Inlaid ruddy twigs, becalmed pine-leaves,*
> > *Air-baubles, and the chain mail of froth . . .*

I notice in the first line of another poem ("Haze, char, and the weather of all souls") what may be an effort at the instant scenic fullness of an opening shot. Move as it may, the picture on the screen gives enviably much at once, and the moviegoing poet,

impatient of his prolix medium, may sometimes try for a light-
ning completeness, a descriptive *coup*. Finally, I wonder if the
first four lines of "An Event" are not indebted to trick
photography:

> *As if a cast of grain leapt back to the hand,*
> *A landscapeful of small black birds, intent*
> *On the far south, convene at some command*
> *At once in the middle of the air . . .*

All of the above is doubtful, but there is no doubt about two
of my poems, "Beasts" and "The Undead." Each owes something
to a particular horror film, in respect of mood, matter, and im-
ages. "Beasts" takes some of its third and fourth stanzas from
Frankenstein Meets the Wolf Man, and "The Undead" obviously
derives in part from Bela Lugosi's *Dracula*. Neither of these
films is great art, though the latter comes close, but both are
good enough to haunt the memory with the double force of
reality and dream, to remind one of a deeper Gothic on which
they draw, and to start the mind building around them. One
would have to be brooding on a film to produce such a visual
pun as "Their black shapes cropped into sudden bats."

THE UNDEAD

> *Even as children they were late sleepers,*
> *Preferring their dreams, even when quick with monsters,*
> *To the world with all its breakable toys,*
> *Its compacts with the dying;*
>
> *From the stretched arms of withered trees*
> *They turned, fearing contagion of the mortal,*

And even under the plums of summer
    Drifted like winter moons.

Secret, unfriendly, pale, possessed
Of the one wish, the thirst for mere survival,
    They came, as all extremists do
        In time, to a sort of grandeur:

Now, to their Balkan battlements
Above the vulgar town of their first lives,
    They rise at the moon's rising. Strange
        That their utter self-concern

Should, in the end, have left them selfless:
Mirrors fail to perceive them as they float
    Through the great hall and up the staircase;
        Nor are the cobwebs broken.

Into the pallid night emerging,
Wrapped in their flapping capes, routinely maddened
    By a wolf's cry, they stand for a moment
        Stoking the mind's eye

With lewd thoughts of the pressed flowers
And bric-a-brac of rooms with something to lose,—
    Of love-dismembered dolls, and children
        Buried in quilted sleep.

Then they are off in a negative frenzy,
Their black shapes cropped into sudden bats
    That swarm, burst, and are gone. Thinking
        Of a thrush cold in the leaves

Who has sung his few summers truly,
Or an old scholar resting his eyes at last,
   We cannot be much impressed with vampires,
      Colorful though they are;

   Nevertheless, their pain is real,
And requires our pity. Think how sad it must be
   To thirst always for a scorned elixir,
      The salt quotidian blood

   Which, if mistrusted, has no savor;
To prey on life forever and not possess it,
   As rock-hollows, tide after tide,
      Glassily strand the sea.

2

The magazine Dreamworks *asked me to testify about the*
dream-element in my writing, and this response appeared
in the Summer 1980 issue. In regard to the dream of my
second paragraph, it now occurs to me that many childhood
visits to Maryland must have made me hazily aware of
the Catoctin Mountains. My remarks were followed by a
reprinting of my long poem "Walking to Sleep."

The "dream aesthetics" in my work would be most obvious
in such a poem as "Walking to Sleep," which derives from a sort
of exploratory dreaming which I experience (and some others,
apparently, do not), or in the later poem "In Limbo," which has
to do with the conversing of all one's selves and ages in the
hypnopompic state. But even where dreaming is not the subject,
I know that the drifting, linking, and swerving of my poetry is

often modelled—even while I strive for a conscious clarity and point—on the flow of consciousness in dream. I also know that it was my own experience as a dreamer which first led me— reading a paperback in a foxhole at Monte Cassino—to sense a submerged pattern of psychic action in the fiction of Poe, about whom I have since written a number of interpretive essays.

You ask for "a dream," and I am not sure whether to give you one which I understand or one which I do not. When I was sixteen, I dreamt of the appearance of an equestrian figure—a cowboy, I think—on the road which led past the gate of the walled vegetable garden and rounded the manure-house behind the barn. The figure gestured to the pine grove across the garden, and to a range of hazy blue mountains, Rockies-like, which had never appeared behind the pine grove before. In a deep, oracular voice, which seemed to be speaking close to my ear, the rider said, "Those are the Old Catica Mountains." I woke up with a feeling of awe, but with no comprehension, and forty years later I feel the same about that comparatively uneventful dream, wherein large and craggy Western forms are glimpsed above a New Jersey farm's horizon. If anyone were to take the first and last syllables of that strange word "Catica," and connect them with the manure-house, I should not thank him for it; a sixteen-year-old boy who has grown up on a farm takes the manure-house for granted, and I did not know the word caca at that age.

Perhaps the old dream still resounds for me (the greatest force is in the words of it) because it was simple and soluble and yet escaped me; by which I mean that my waking mind never came to share it. A similar dream, a bit more than a decade later, was understood at once, enjoyed, and put away amongst fathomed experiences. At that time I was busy in left-wing politics, and not long before the dream had helped a young woman gather a great quantity of articles which were to be auctioned for the benefit of a radical organization. One item was a mantilla, which the young woman tried on, and which rather became her. The organization, by the way, was ostensibly concerned with relief for anti-Franco exiles and the like. A short time after the auction, during a house-party at Wellfleet, I behaved somewhat improperly toward the young woman, and afterward did not feel easy about it. The dream which summed all this up had no visual content which I can remember; what it amounted to was a resonant voice which intoned, just as I was waking up, "The Spanish Cape Mystery!" There was a mystery novel of that title knocking around our apartment at the time; the author, I believe, was Ellery Queen. It will be seen, however, that the title served, within my dream, to recall the Spanish civil war, the mantilla, the furtiveness of "front-group" politics, Cape Cod, and such guilt as I felt about the girl. Its effect was to remind me of something in a veiled manner; at the same time, the reminder was so tricky and portentous as to amount to a recommendation that something be recognized and then laughed off.

One more dream, which seems to me both hilarious and embarrassing, because I cannot bear self-pity or feelings of nobility in myself. This dream occurred at a time when I had been, as they say, "pressing myself very hard," and apparently felt that I was neglecting my own work or pleasure for the sake of others. In the dream I was standing in a highway some distance from a little town. A steam-roller, driven by myself, came toward me as I stood there, and my spirit therefore prudently flew up and looked down on the goings-on. When the steam-roller had passed over my body, it lay in the road like a rolled-out ginger cookie; it was not, however, light-brown in color, as gingerbread-men are, but was full of red and blue traceries resembling the representations of innards in medical books. Whereupon, like a piece of wrapping paper driven by a gale, my body was peeled from the road surface and whipped across intervening fields to the village, where it at once became a stained-glass window in a church. I believe that this dream requires no explanation, but I report it because, though emotionally disgraceful, it is visually clever and delightful.

Forewords

I

The first of these two forewords appeared in Strong
Measures *(1986), a selection of "contemporary American
poetry in traditional forms" edited by Philip Dacey and
David Jauss.*

SOME OF the crudity with which we discuss matters of artistic form has to do with politics; and there have, in fact, been moments of history in which an artist's choice of form was a clear political statement. The "picturesque" mode of landscape gardening was, as the writings of its advocates show, antiauthoritarian in its simulation of wild and "untamed" nature; it was opposed to the geometric constraints of, let us say, Versailles. Stendhal reflects this politicization of gardening in the second chapter of *The Red and the Black*, where we learn from an indignant Liberal that M. de Rênal, the mayor of Verrières and the embodiment of "despotic" repression, annually causes the plane-trees of the town to be trimmed and pollarded. In 1831, Stendhal and his reader knew precisely the social overtones, *for them*, of formal regularity in horticulture; but in the present century, such explicit significance has faded from park and garden, or become at most a matter of individual response. Forms, in other words, survive their moments of social or other bearing and become mere available instruments of expression.

It does not seem to me that, at the present moment, the

assignment of definite meaning or effect to poetic forms can be very persuasive. To be sure, there are people who associate meter and rhyme with order and good sense, or denounce them as affected and reactionary; there are those who regard free verse as sincere and forward-looking, and those who dismiss it as squalidly prosaic. But not much of that blather holds up if we look at what has actually been written in this century, and at what is being written now. Was populism more at home in the jaunty measures of Vachel Lindsay, or in the loose chants of Carl Sandburg? One could readily think of twenty similar questions about modern and contemporary verse, questions which would destroy themselves in the asking. The fact is that no form belongs inevitably with any theme or attitude; no form is good or appropriate in itself, but any form can be *made* good by able hands.

If a number of poets are now turning toward meter and stanza and the like, it may be a near-sufficient explanation to recall Yeats's notion that in art, as in all things, impulses exhaust themselves and give way to counter-impulses. That is, a number of contemporary poets may simply be tired of what they and others have been doing, and in their assault upon sameness they may be finding challenge and refreshment in neglected technical resources. The attraction is not merely to formal means, I should guess, but toward some new scope and style. Both attractions and rejections, in art, have always involved more than form. I think, for example, of certain poets who, a few decades back, made war upon "the sonnet." These militants were not, actually, objecting to a fourteen-line paradigm having a number of possible rhyme-schemes. Their true objection was to how that form (and others) was being used by a group of accomplished and well-known lyricists, who dealt perhaps too exclusively in passionate love, natural beauty, and a vocabulary of breathless words like "riant." The issue was not merely form but also, and far more importantly, vision and lexicon. The sonnet survives all attacks and misuses, of course; it does so as a possible arrangement of materials, and as such may say, "before poetry was, I am." It also survives because in many ages—the twenties and eighties included—it has proven a valid instrument for an extraordinary diversity of poets.

Barry Goldensohn, addressing the question of why "revolutions" in English-language poetry always take the form of a supposed return to "the language of ordinary men," finds the cause in Shakespeare: the influence of our greatest poet has, he thinks, repeatedly moved us to repudiate any too-elaborate style and move in the direction of a dramatic poetry based upon "real speech." That is probably right. If so, I should describe the last two decades as a time of widespread "revolution" in which, despite lively individual achievements, the prevalent styles have been mistakenly closer to flat declarative talk than to dramatic poetry, a mode in which "real speech" is always honed, charged, and heightened by artifice. I hope that a persistence or resurgence of metrical writing, and of artifice in general, will now restore some lost force and expressive capability to American poetry.

If that happens, many poets will learn by experience that good rhyme is not ornament but emphasis, ligature, and significant sound; that a good poet is not coerced by any technical means, however demanding they may be; that one does not set out to write a quatrain, but, rather, finds that one is doing so. And so on. Without being contentious—without denying the merits of Whitman, say, or Williams—I send my particularly good wishes to poets who think this a time for strong measures.

2

At Alan Newman's invitation, I wrote the following for
New England Reflections *(1981), a volume of the Howes*
brothers' turn-of-the-century photographs.

If you live in this part of New England, the pictures taken
by the Howes brothers of Ashfield can give you a momentarily
jumbled sense of time. That is because so much of western
Massachusetts and its periphery has proved unimprovable, and
looks something as it did eighty or ninety years ago. There is
never any doubt, to be sure, that in turning these pages one is
looking into the past; it is a horse-drawn, unpaved, and largely
unmechanized world that one sees, and the decor and clothing
are a dead giveaway. Still, if today you turn off the big highways
anywhere in Howes territory and let the roads rise, twist, and
narrow amidst trees and stone walls, you will soon see the ge-
neric house which the brothers so frequently recorded. It is a
rather stark clapboard house, perhaps with a narrow front porch
and a shed and barn adjoining. You would not say that the
grounds had been landscaped, though the old rock maples are
beautiful; there may be a bit of litter about—a board, a barrow,
an overturned tub which seems to have been there a while. A
grape arbor, very likely; a garden, an orchard, stony fields. Be-
hind all, you will see for certain the wooded hills as they always
were, their dark conifer patches striated with birch, and above
them a sky which knows how to be cold in season. Some social
scientist tells us that 85 percent of Americans now live in city
or suburb, in much-changed or developed communities where
the awareness of topography is dimmed. What would a Dallasite
recognize in a picture of old Dallas? But certain pictures in the

Howes archive convey to me an odd first impression of familiar vistas infiltrated by strangers.

One reason why Howes photography can affect you so is that it has none of the haze and chiaroscuro of memory, of history; though pointedly composed, the pictures take in everything on equal terms, and the least detail comes forward sharply. That tangle of elderberry, fox grape, and wild cherry is just down our road on the right-hand side, this minute; that sledgehammer standing on its head by a wall is the image of mine. Another reason for the partial illusion of presentness is that the people, with their period air and attire, are so often subordinated to representations of structures and farmsteads, of interiors, of enterprises, of groups and of group labor. I am told that the Howes brothers' advance man, going from town to town, secured commissions for the recording of family, commercial, or institutional history; when the photographer came, it was not to do impressions of the landscape or portraits of isolate heads, but to record milieus, gatherings, whole aspects of the world's work. These photographs are of a special sort, then—documentary in intention, answering the customer's desire, displaying people in the midst of their settings and undertakings. Old family albums of the time, or the products of portrait studios, would give us other glimpses of the same world; but these, I think, have something more or different to tell.

In good light, the Howes camera could take a fifth-of-a-second exposure, so that the catatonic expressions of an earlier day were not necessary. Nevertheless, it is fairly seldom that these faces, which look as a rule toward the camera, are smiling or projecting personality. Eight bundled-up men and women, about to push off for a bobsled ride, are full of gaiety and expectation; seated on his front stoop with his shoes on a city sidewalk, a solid man with a well-fed family, a derby, bow tie, and watch chain, lets us know that he is an aggressive man of business; two stylish adolescent boys with knotted scarves are the only subjects, in the pictures I happen to have sampled, who regard the lens with a sleek and amused complacency. On the lawn behind them is a hammock emblematic of leisure. Most convey little of polish or well-to-do ease. A wedding party in a pasture is uniformly grave, though the bride's ducked head may be hiding a shy smile; the grandmother giving an infant its bottle is frowningly blank; dwarfed by a barnlike house at the corner of Pine Street, a family stares at us with expressionless faces. Is it diffidence we see in such cases? Stoicism? A lingering Calvinist austerity? Possibly, but I think also of what one of the Adamses said—that the pitiful thing is not to be poor, but to feel that one does not matter. Surely, to face a camera, especially a professional one, was not an everyday thing for some of these folk. I suspect that their seriousness of mien has often to do with a sense that their lives for once are going on record, that, however modestly, they are entering history.

Am I permitted one more catalogue? In these studies not of single selves but of interrelated lives and their properties, there is a wish to *show* as much as possible; the whole family and its homestead, with the horse and wagon on display; the grade-school class putting forward the potted plants they have tended; the man who, torn between exhibiting his work and its fruits, wears a Sunday suit and hat while holding a calf on a halter; the busy barbershop seen *in toto,* from the front door clear to the shelved bottles in the back; the tobacco workers showing the process of rolling the cheesecloth after the harvest; the timber gang showing you how they work together. Workers, in these pictures, are generally more at ease than those who have nothing to do but pose, but the salient thing about them is not personality but function: this is a man, you say, who is proud of his axe-work; there is a fellow who can use a peavey. Perhaps the height of personal effacement is the photo of a man who has somehow managed to get a yardful of leashed dogs to hold still; the one thing blurred is his face.

Some of the descendants of the Howes brothers' subjects have doubtless enjoyed this century's mobility, its pursuit of self-fulfillment, its softer and glossier ways of living. Having had their pictures taken amidst the pigeons of the Piazza di San Marco, they may look with little yearning on the pages of this book. Still, what we mostly see here is a self-respecting breed who knew how to do many things, who knew who they were, who made themselves comfortable enough, who had their recreations, were more cohesive than we, and were closer than we to a sometimes hard but always beautiful land. It is not a bad picture.

For several years, it was my job to say some initial words at the May ceremonials of the American Academy of Arts and Letters. Here are two samples, from 1977 and 1978 respectively.

Opening Remarks

I

LADIES AND GENTLEMEN: Often, at about this point in our program, someone says a good word for art. We all think highly of arts and letters, or we wouldn't be here. But precisely because we know something about art we take no pleasure in hearing it gushingly and outrageously praised, and I shall try to avoid that in these remarks. I promise, for example, not to proclaim that the artist is ahead of his time; that he inhabits a superior reality; or that, God being dead, the artist must take His place.

Except for Wallace Stevens, I can think of no excellent artist of our time who has made much of the notion that art can take the place of religion; and I think, frankly, that Stevens's ascetic poetry implies not so much a heightened expectation of art as a diminished or diffident expectation of life. As a rule, our best artists don't make grand claims for what they do, and often they show their love of art by chastening it. You all know Marianne Moore's poem about poetry which begins, "I too dislike it," and goes on to say, "there are things that are important beyond all this fiddle." Louise Bogan, in one of her early letters to Edmund Wilson, says flatly, "I do not care for literature, as such." And Auden, in a poem about music, once said:

. . . these halcyon structures are useful
As structures go—though not to be confused
With anything really important
Like feeding strays or looking pleased when caught
By a bore or a hideola . . .

That's from a poem called "Music is International," in which Auden praises music as a great universal language which by its very nature urges a joyous concord; and yet, he says, it matters less than small actual deeds of decency and kindness.

Having chastened art by means of these quotations, let me try to make modest amends. It is surely nonsense to say that the artist is ahead of his time; the maker of any art object knows that its time is now. If art attains to prophecy, it does so in the special sense defined by R. G. Collingwood. "The artist must prophesy," Collingwood said, "not in the sense that he foretells things to come, but in the sense that he tells the audience, at the risk of their displeasure, the secrets of their own hearts." The audience, as we know, is often displeased, and slow to accept the revelations of art. And that, I think, is what Jean Cocteau means by saying, "When a work of art appears to be in advance of its period, it is really the period that has lagged behind the work of art." It seems to me that the job of art is continually to test all of our languages, discovering what words and concepts are truly alive for us, what patterns may be made in good conscience, what sounds, forms, colors, and volumes can honestly express us as we now are. Such findings are attended, for those who can bear them, by the by-products of beauty and joy. Whether or not people like it, the job of art must forever be done, because people and societies cannot afford to be ignorant of what they feel. We honor today a number

of people who have served art, and our common life, in this
essential way.

2

Ladies and Gentlemen: Samuel Johnson once said, "What is
written without effort is in general read without pleasure," and
of course the statement could be applied not only to writing
but to all the arts. I've sometimes quoted that sentence of Dr.
Johnson's in recent years, particularly to students of writing, and
I've been interested to notice that many people frown when they
hear it. What is it that they don't like? I'm going to make three
guesses.

For one thing, some people doubtless feel that pleasure is
too trifling a word for what art bestows. They'd rather talk of
truth, of vision, of the clarification of life. The answer to that
is that art can give all those things, and also give pleasure in
the process; to be enjoyable is not necessarily to be trivial. A
more valid reservation might come from the sort of people who
think of art in terms of progress and experiment, and who are
willing, in concert hall or gallery, to endure confusion and do
without pleasure if only they believe a work to be significant
and forward-looking. It's admirable, I think, to be open to the
new, and willing to learn; I submit, however, that once one has
adjusted to the new, it must give pleasure or it will not be art.
Even when a work is difficult in style or terrible in meaning, its
office, as Ezra Pound said, is "to make glad the heart of man"
by proving once again that our experience can be confronted
and handsomely embodied.

I suspect that there's a second thing in Johnson's sentence
with which some might differ—its clear implication that the

artist can govern the response of his reader or hearer or viewer.
We appear to be living in an age which has excitedly rediscov-
ered subjectivity, and one gets the impression, from some
French critics, that the thing to do with a work of art is to
fantasize and free-associate in its presence. For some years now,
in America, certain professors have been using "structured" as
a cuss-word and "open-ended" as a term of approval; it has been
said that the artist should not impose himself upon his work
and its public, but should imitate nature—nature in this case
meaning not the beehive or the sand dollar or human nature
but the indeterminacy of subatomic particles. That this kind of
thinking still thrives is indicated by the continual appearance of
new jargon. The other day, a student showed me a vague and
fragmentary contemporary poem, and praised it for being "un-
manipulative." It certainly was. The best answer to these atti-
tudes, it seems to me, is the existence of such occasions as this.
We wouldn't be here if it weren't clear to us that there is better
art, and worse art, and that there may be such a thing as mas-
tery. Whatever mastery may signify, one thing it surely means
is that the master artist, however intricate or subtle his concep-
tions, channels our reactions and forcefully limits our freedom
to misunderstand him.

Finally, I suppose that Johnson's emphasis on effort may
sound a little grim in an age which so prizes spontaneity. We
all relish the spontaneous, and dislike whatever is labored; but
I do think that in recent decades spontaneity has often been
misconceived, and that many have exaggerated the aesthetic ad-
vantages of going off half-cocked. To be sure, one can think of
splendid cases of swift conception, as in jazz improvisations or
the brush paintings of the Japanese; but such successes are
based upon long discipline, practice, and tradition. It does

appear that most good art, even though it may seem quick and impulsive, arises in part from hard work, present or past. I think of Emerson, because I have just been reading him. He is our national prophet of spontaneity, and the prose of his essays is full of leaps and swerves and abrupt discoveries, giving an exciting sense of the immediate, and of the mind in action. Yet the scholars tell us that Emerson was incapable of anything impromptu and that he was a pack rat of his own thoughts and phrases, who rummaged in his notebooks for the materials of his poems and lectures, and pillaged his lectures in the making of his essays. He was not, in short, a blurter, and his patient achievement suggests a definition of the best kind of spontaneity—that in which the artist, while laboring to compose and deepen his ideas, at the same time artfully retrieves the suddenness and surprise with which they first came to him.

All of which leads me to say that what we do on this agreeable day is to thank a number of artists for taking the trouble to produce works both deliberate and fresh, works which awaken our imaginations, and shape them, and give us pleasure.

The magazine Translation *solicited a number of brief essays,
this of mine among them, for its tenth anniversary issue in
Spring of 1984.*

Notes on Translating
Classic Verse Plays

A PLAY, like any other literary form, may be translated with
the solitary reader in mind; that was, I think, my main initial
notion in 1952 when I went to work on *The Misanthrope*. If the
audience is imagined as one person in a chair, the translator
takes the literacy and taste of his reader for granted and con-
centrates on using the English language, in its best present con-
dition, to approximate the art and substance of an ancient or
foreign original. But if it occurs to him during that process (as
it shortly did to me) that the translation might also prove to be
an actable script, he is suddenly to some extent involved in the
collaborative world of a performing art, and is writing not only
for the individual reader but for rows of strangers in orchestra,
balcony, and box.

The fact is, however, that the exciting thought of stage
production did not confuse my aims as a translator of *The
Misanthrope*. Already, though I had had a very limited experi-
ence of the theater, I knew some actors capable of handling the
language and formal conventions of such a play, and I had seen
them use high artifice and make their audiences respond. There
was no temptation to ask less of actors than Molière had done.
It did not strike me that the play needed interjected explanations
(of the judicial system, for instance, or of the Marshalsea), or
that it should be condescendingly "adapted" to a possible con-
temporary audience. Since the theme of the play was timeless,

there was no call to make *The Misanthrope* timely by "updating" of any kind. In short, it never seriously occurred to me to doctor the play (even had I known how) for the purposes of the current stage. Happily, the Poets Theatre production (Cambridge, 1955) and that at Theatre East (New York, 1956) proved that a comic classic belonging to a related culture can be faithfully presented to the satisfaction of a modern American audience.

Not for a moment had I thought of dispensing, as many now would do, with English equivalents of Molière's meter and rhyme. There is a thoroughly crazy recent idea, sometimes held by bright people, that we have put meter and rhyme forever behind us, and that non-English literature embodied in traditional means must speak to us, if at all, through some "free" or prosaic period style. I am reminded of a man I met who was taking religious instruction and who complained of his instructor, "He ain't trying to convert me to Christianity; he's trying to convert Christianity to *me*." Why Molière's couplets must be preserved I have elsewhere said in part: to make it inescapably clear when any speech modulates into the parody-tragical; to include high comedy and farce in the one music; to make deliberate repetitions of ideas sound resourceful (as they are) rather than verbose; to phase the distinct stages of *tirades* which, prosaically rendered, would seem prolix. Let me offer now another reason or two for the preservation of the couplet. Molière wrote more than thirty pieces for the stage, of which the least familiar to us are not so much plays as they are entertainments involving music and dance. If we revise our sense of Molière's theatrical scope by scanning his whole *oeuvre*, it becomes quite reasonable to look for elements of the "operatic" or "balletic" in his verse plays. Eliante's charming speech in Act Two of *The Misanthrope*, in which she tells how "lovers manage, in their passion's cause/ To love their ladies even for their flaws," is a spoken aria, and would be far less clearly such without measure and rhyme. The lovers' quarrel between Valère and Mariane, in the presence of Dorine (*Tartuffe*, II, iv), is so thoroughly balletic as to prescribe the successive positions and movements of all three characters, in symmetries which are stressed (as prose or prosaic verse could not do) when the dialogue rises to stichomythia or balancing couplets. Not to see this sort of thing, in armchair or theater seat, is to lack a full sense of Molière's theater.

Are there any disadvantages to paralleling Molière's form? One only, and that hardly sufficient to outweigh the advantages. A recent article quoted an anonymous theater figure as saying that my translations take some of the "darkness" out of Molière. If my critic is the sort of person who wishes Tartuffe to be an enigmatic colossus of evil, a Frankenstein's monster rather than a character among characters, then his quarrel is not with me but with Molière. If he thinks that I have softened Molière's speeches, I can only add that better Molièrists than I have found them accurate enough in thought and in tone. But if he means that English rhyming is more emphatic than French rhyming, so that a translation into English couplets will more often have the whip-crack sound of joke or epigram than the original did, I must own that he is right. Formal fidelity entails that slight and unavoidable infidelity. I don't think that too terribly much darkness is lost thereby.

Other playwrights require other choices, or other grounds for choice. In attempting Racine's *Andromache*, I felt once again that the translator should work in English couplets, but this time chiefly for the reason that rhyming measures, in that play, help to express a glorious but superficial order of society to which the violent passions of the principals are indifferent. Given that rationale, and given the play's tragic mode, it seemed obvious that certain effects of rhyme appropriate to Molière must at all costs be avoided in rendering Racine. I sought to avoid all tricky conspicuousness, minimized the use of feminine endings, and did not shy away from such obvious rhymes (*hate* and *fate*, for example) as the play's spare and insistent lexicon demanded. I hope to have got away with it.

I began by saying that, at the beginning of my efforts as a play translator, I was aware of the possibility of stage presentation but did not modify my treatment of the text on that account. Since then I have hung around theaters a good deal, watching various kinds of plays take shape, and have found that, even if one translates from such thoroughly verbal playwrights as Molière and Racine, there is much to be learned by watching actors and directors. One may learn, for one thing, to imagine with what pace, pitch, and "build" a good actor might attack a particular speech, and thus select, from alternative "faithful" wordings of its thought, the most sayable and actable. Sometimes this will involve discovering a character's specific English rhythm—the spluttering, hypertense cadences, for instance, of Arnolphe in *School for Wives*. Another thing one may learn is that a character, though given no lines to say, can by his or her mere presence powerfully affect the mood and action of a scene. One may learn that, when exposition is particularly compressed (as sometimes in Racine), one should not forbid oneself a clarifying phrase for the audience's sake, provided it does not derail or detain the thought. One can learn, too, that it is best not to translate the dialogue of servants into thoroughgoing cockney, Brooklynese, Northern Farmer, or what have you; if one provides simplicity and a little bad grammar, the rest may be left to actor and director. As for directors, the good ones are very instructive and the bad ones—the ones with vile "fresh concepts," who like to put their stamp on things—encourage the translator to produce a text inviolably exact and clear.

My friend Edwin Honig and I recorded a conversation which became a part of his excellent book on translation, The Poet's Other Voice *(1985).*

A Talk about Translation

EH   I was reading the introduction to your translations of *The Misanthrope* and *Tartuffe*, and I noticed you said about the necessity of using the couplet that *The Misanthrope* required it because the work is so epigrammatic, while *Tartuffe* is less so.

RW   Yes. I think there are fewer moments of deliberate wit in *Tartuffe*, and so the requirement that one keep rhyme and meter for the sake of epigrammatic snap is a little less. Still, there's a good deal of that quality in anything that Molière wrote, so I wouldn't think of putting any of his verse plays into prose.

EH   Even though he was not a poet outside of the plays?

RW   Very little, I think. He did (I believe) write a number of lyrics and some little verses, but no, he wasn't really a poet outside of the plays, and inside the poetic plays he's a very prosaic poet in many respects. I guess I said in one of the introductions that, by contrast to someone like Racine, he's almost free of figurative language: he also doesn't use key words, thematic words, in the vigorous way that Racine does, although some mistaken critic, I suppose, might want to argue about that with me. In any case, it makes Molière much easier to translate than Racine would be, not merely because he's comedy (and somehow rhyme consorts more readily with comedy than tragedy) but also because you don't have to wrestle with difficult figures and key words quite so much.

EH   There are many interesting things about those translations that I would like to come back to a little later. Meanwhile, may I ask what your original contact with the idea of translation was?

That is, how you conceived of it when you started. Not neces-
sarily with Molière, but earlier. I know you did other things
earlier.

RW I think my first experience with translation was when
André du Bouchet, who's now a rather well-established French
poet, and I, were fellow graduate students at Harvard. I had
picked up enough French from basic courses, and reading, and
being in France during World War II, so that I felt able to make
a start on most French poems. So I would sit around with
André, trying to translate his poems into English, and he sat
around trying to translate mine into French. And it was a nice
way to begin one's career as a translator. Not that I did anything
that was any good, but knowing André I was able to begin the
translation of any one of his poems with a sense that I knew
his tones of voice and his preoccupations.

EH What you say immediately strikes a chord because now,
almost every time I've spoken with a poet who's translated, there
has been an experience of working with someone at the begin-
ning, whether a friend or an inciting informant. In the case of
Ben Belitt, who began with Wallace Fowlie, the challenge was
to please his informant, who was interested in the early modern
poets—Rimbaud particularly—who hadn't been translated very
well. So that the relationship was the immediate instigation not
only to do the translations but also to do them very well.

RW I suppose that, Fowlie being a translator of the French
himself, they must have been vying a little bit. They were having
a *concours*, weren't they?

EH Well, I don't know what the circumstances were. I had the
impression that Fowlie wanted verse translations that stood up
on their own. Whether he had done Rimbaud in verse or prose,
I don't know. Later on Belitt worked on other poets, but in this

connection he got to know some of them personally. This was the stimulus for him to do Neruda, for example.

RW He got to know Neruda personally? Yes, I think that's terribly important. I couldn't imagine beginning to translate anybody living or dead without at least having the illusion of some kind of personal understanding—some understanding of the range of his feelings beyond the particular work. That's hard, of course, in the case of someone like du Bellay, one of whose poems I recently translated. But even in his case I did develop an adequate sense of background and of the emotional set in which the poem was made.

EH Does that mean that you almost always translate from poets you have a sense of identity with?

RW Yes, I think so. I suspect I have to like the poem pretty well in the first place. This keeps me, I think, from being a professional translator—doing things wholesale. I have to like the poem and feel it has something to do with my feelings—that I understand the feelings that went into it. Perhaps, also, I like it and am particularly well motivated when I feel the poem represents, as it were, an extension or stretching of my own emotional possibilities.

EH You emphasize something that Belitt also suggested as a prime motivation for doing the poem—pleasure, pleasure in doing it, rather than gain, but gain as it might happen through pleasure.

RW Monetary gain is always unexpected, I suppose, in the translation business, though I imagine it's better paid now than it used to be, isn't it?

EH I don't know.

RW But you don't think of pay... at any rate, someone like me who translates individual poems by different people out of various languages is obviously not proceeding in a businesslike manner. I'm just responding to things that catch my eye or have been brought to my attention. Sometimes people who have a feeling for what I'm like, or what my work is like, are fairly accurate about prescribing what I should attempt. For example, Simon Karlinsky wrote me a while back about doing a number of poems by the exiled Russian poet Nikolai Morshen, since he saw some affinities too; Karlinsky is a very good finger man. I found Max Hayward to be similarly gifted in matching the translator to the poem. The Voznesensky poems that he and Patricia Blake once picked out for me to do were pretty much the right ones.

EH   I see. Well, that goes along with other incidents of the same kind I know about. I want to go back now to your beginnings as a translator. Your first experience translating had to do with the poems of a friend, the French poet du Bouchet. Then, after that, what happened?

RW   I think my early efforts at translation had largely to do with the French, because that was the only foreign language of which I possessed anything; though of that I had a very faulty knowledge, and still do.

EH   It was school French?

RW   School French fortified by the French a soldier picks up during war experience. I remember translating some little poems of Villiers de l'Isle-Adam, an author to whom du Bouchet had directed my attention. I had an anthology of great old chestnuts of the French tradition, and found in it an ode of La Fontaine's that appealed to me a good deal and . . .

EH   You just picked these out, as you were looking through.

RW   . . . just picked them out. As they say—they grabbed me. Having done La Fontaine's "Ode to Pleasure," I asked Harry

Levin to see if I'd gotten the words right. He kindly helped me
as he had helped Marianne Moore . . . or perhaps was to help; I
forget at what time he began to help her with her French trans-
lations. He was always generous with that kind of aid. I tried to
do a little Catullus around 1949 or so, but I had no luck with
it. I can't stand the mincing and evasive translations of his
tougher poems that one has in the Loeb Library; at the same
time I couldn't find a way to be nasty in a language that was
poetically effective.

EH Why did you want to translate Catullus?

RW I'd always been fascinated by particular tones of his. He
does not seem to me to be a terribly broad sensibility, but a
great deal of personality transpires from his poetry as it does,
say, from Villon—another example of a person who is not very
broad but is very strong.

EH Then the kind of interest you developed in translation
came from similar desultory lookings into books and advice from
people who wrote you or asked you to do it.

RW Well, the askings came later, after I'd done a certain num-
ber of poems, more or less by accident. That is, through falling
in love with them myself or through having someone say, "Have
a look at this." I suppose I began to be invited to do poems in
translation after I had done *The Misanthrope* translation, which
was published in 1955. People began to think of me as an avail-
able translator—someone who, with a little linguistic aid, might
do things out of languages he didn't know.

EH So that was the first significant translation you did.

RW Yes. There are translations sprinkled through my second
book, *Ceremony*, and my third book, *Things of This World*. But
there aren't too many of them, really. I suppose I began to be
thought of as a laborer in that vineyard when *The Misanthrope*

came out. . . . I must qualify that. I do remember now that when I was living out in the town of Corrales, New Mexico, which we both know so well, Jackson Mathews wrote me and said he was putting together for New Directions a collection of *The Flowers of Evil* of Baudelaire, and that he wasn't quite satisfied with the existing versions of the great chestnut poems, the "Invitation to the Voyage," "Correspondences," and "The Albatross." He asked me to try them. So I tried them. That was 1952.

EH   Did you feel that you had *done* the job—that is, was he satisfied with them?

RW   He was satisfied with them, though I remember Jack saying that my reaching for a rhyme in the "Correspondences" poem had obliged me to refer to a "child's caress" in a way that would have offended Baudelaire's fastidiousness. But he liked them all right and used them in that anthology. And I was satisfied with "L'Invitation au voyage." Though I thought, "Of course, it's a failure," I thought that it was a less ludicrous failure than the attempts of others.

EH   Yes, one has to measure one's success by the failures of others, even of one's own. One of the things that interests me in the translation of poetry is the way a very scrupulous translator who has a strong poetic voice of his own (and I think you fit this description) cannot escape merging his voice with that of the poet he is translating. What do you feel? Do you deliberately try to suppress your own style in translating?

RW   I think that I do try to avoid putting into anyone else's poem, as I bring it across into English, mannerisms of my own, and I certainly try to efface myself as much as possible. I shouldn't like to seem to be demonstrating that Voznesensky could write like Wilbur if he'd only try. What I say to myself— not too dishonestly, I hope—is that I'm putting whatever abilities I have at the service of the poem I'm translating, and that because I feel some kind of affinity with him, or at least with the particular work I'm rendering, that I *can* use such words as readily come to me without imposing myself on the work. I can give an example of this. I can contrast myself with Ezra Pound in this respect. Ezra Pound translated Voltaire's poem to Madame du Châtelet, turning it into a kind of imagistic prose poem. Some of the effects are quite brilliant and charming. He takes everything that is abstract and makes it concrete. When there's a reference to love, for example, capitalized Love (and Voltaire is really thinking of statues of Eros in a garden), Pound puts lovers on the grass.

EH   Where they belong.

RW   Yes. I translated the same poem, trying—without using antique language, without sounding eighteenth-century—to transmit it purely, both regarding the language and regarding the form. I discovered in the process that he kept shifting his rhyme pattern in the quatrain he was using, and where he was unfaithful to his own precedent I followed him; even went that far. Faithful to his infidelities.

EH   You were conscious of Pound's translation when doing yours.

RW   I had seen it, but it was so different an effort from mine that it couldn't possibly have influenced me. At the same time I wasn't writing a rebuke to Pound—he was doing an imagist exercise upon the basis of a Voltaire poem.

EH   Yes.

RW   I was trying to persuade myself that I was bringing the poem alive into English with no additions of my own. I know that any such belief is an illusion, but the pursuit of the illusion can bring one closer to the fact, I think. I know that when I first tried to do some poems from the Spanish, which I don't really understand—I'm particularly prone to error when I'm doing Spanish because I know some Italian and get betrayed by cognates—even with linguistic assistance, I still manage to make blunders. When I found that I had made mistakes, I did my best to iron them out, in the light of criticism. But when the first Guillén translation was published I can remember friends saying, "That's a nice Wilbur poem, strongly influenced by Jorge Guillén." I had no such sense of it, and was distressed.

EH   It might be that when you translate a contemporary this is more likely to happen. Perhaps when you translate du Bellay or Voltaire, where the language is not contemporary, the effect is different. But I wanted to ask you, in connection with what you said about Pound regarding his translation as an exercise in imagist writing, do you regard individual translations of single poems as exercises of a sort? I don't mean translations of plays now.

RW   I find that I feel a kind of abhorrence for the word *exercise*, even though in teaching poetry I ask my students, if they feel like it, to do this or that kind of exercise which I propose. No, I have a feeling that though I am not writing a poem of my own, I am not merely lubricating my muscles, as it were, when I bring somebody else's poem into English. I feel as though I were doing something complete, the purpose of which lies within itself.

EH   You don't feel that sense of substitution for doing your own work that Lowell talks about in his apologia for *Imitations*.

RW   One or two things I've said have betrayed an awareness that I'm drawn to a poem because it's partly me and partly not me. Because to write it in English will seem to extend me emotionally. In that sense I have a personal interest in what is being done, and I am in that sense writing another poem of my own. Since I am following as carefully as I can the thoughts and feelings of someone close yet different, it's very likely going to have consequences for the next poem I write.

EH   You sense that?

RW   Yes.

EH   As you're working or afterwards?

RW   Oh, afterwards. I don't think that I would ever undertake a job of translation out of an expectation of what it would do for me as a writer, or for the purpose of keeping my hand in. But I do know, in retrospect, that by Englishing 1,800 lines of a Molière play I've doomed myself for some months thereafter to cast my thoughts in couplets—at least initially. For better or worse, ideas propose themselves in couplets for quite a while after I've done such a job.

EH   Well, this then is a kind of fate—after translation. Working off a high. I spoke to John Hollander about his experiences as a translator and he mentioned Yiddish poets with whom he had to work. Because he didn't actually know Yiddish, he had to learn some and check with Irving Howe, on a poet of Russian origin named Halpern. He said this was a very significant experience for him because in doing the work he found he was able to extend his voice in such a way that after doing Halpern his own work changed—expanded in its possibilities, I take it.

RW   I'm sure it's that way. Think of it on the children's playground level, where some little classmate says to you, "I dare you to say such and such a forbidden word," and you say it at once. At *his* urging. You're more capable of saying it on your own impulse thereafter.

EH   So there's an extension and expansion, at least potentially, in one's work as a translator. It isn't only that one does it for pleasure, but the pleasure is really the potentiality of growing in one's own work.

RW   Though I think, speaking for myself, that I would always hide any such motive from myself in the process of writing, I know that it's one of the rewards of translating.

EH   Very good. I'm very interested in that. I think we should go back to the Molière plays. You did three of them.

RW   Yes, and I'm now working on a fourth. I didn't think I was going to do four, but I've gotten drawn into *Les femmes savantes,* and am now approaching the end of the first act. So I suppose I'll go on to the end.

EH   Are you doing this one in the same way you did the others?

RW   Yes, and of course by now it does go faster. I know how to do it, much more surely than when I began with *The Misanthrope,* around 1952. At the same time, there are a few obstacles that arise when one is doing a fourth Molière play. Though Molière shamelessly reproduced his own rhymes and situations, I feel hesitant to use once again the same rhymes by which I solved the couplets of the other three plays I have done. That's silly, but I nevertheless feel it.

EH   Are only certain rhymes possible or ideally any number of them?

RW   Given a coercive text that wants you to reproduce it as exactly as possible, and given what amounts to repeated vaude-ville situations, one finds that the poverty of rhyme in English becomes painful; and even though Molière has, in dealing with the same comic situations, used the same words, I find myself wishing that in my own role I didn't have to. That lengthens the task.

EH   It's a fine psychological matter. I wonder if it has to do with your being a modern poet who doesn't like to repeat himself, or whether it has to do with your not being essentially a professional playwright, in the way Molière was, who would know the value of the stock and type things that work in theater. *RW* I'm sure that both of those things would be true. I expect that most poets who choose to rhyme, nowadays, are troubled about using easy rhymes and are embarrassed about using their own rhymes more than once.

EH Yes.

RW It extends also, I suppose, to the whole vocabulary. I can remember Dick Eberhart saying to me once about a poem of mine that satisfied me very much, "You've used that word before!"

EH Oh, God. Like a member of the family who knows all your bad habits.

RW Yes.

EH Well, rhyme is the essence of your translations of Molière. In some way it's what makes for the dramatic element as well as keeps the poetry going. I'm not sure I'm able to explain what I mean when I say, "It makes for the dramatic element," because one would think that rhyme would *stop* dramatic happening or would be an artifice that was too transparent.

RW I think the transparency and prosaic quality of so much of the language keeps the rhyme from seeming too artificial. And also, the flow of Molière's speech, his tendency not to close every couplet, makes it possible for rhyme to attain its chief effect as provider of poetic emphasis. And also as a sign of the stages of an argument: one of the things I've noticed is that, in the very best prose translations of these verse plays of Molière, the long speeches seem infinitely too long. That is because the steps and the stages are not in the prose demarcated by measures and rhymes.

EH   He has a number of long speeches.

RW   Lots of *tirades,* yes.

EH   I suppose that one of the things that strikes an English reader about rhyme in verse plays, where our tradition is unrhymed iambic pentameter, is the fact that in other traditions one can get so much out of a simple and very basic kind of rhyme—I mean in foreign-language plays. In Spanish, for example, almost any playwright writing in Molière's time would be engaged in doing a play where there are about eight or ten different verse forms possible, and each used formulaically according to the kind of emotion or the kind of situation, usually quite stock, that is being prepared.

RW   So there would be a rough analogy to grand opera.

EH   Yes. But of course it's impossible to reproduce in translation, though it's been attempted in the nineteenth century. One would expect to find a greater variety in such drama, just as, I suppose, one wonders that a musical tune, a complicated one, can be played on a simple stringed instrument, which may have only one string, like the *gusle,* say. There must be something there having to do with the way the form is traditionally maneuvered.

RW   You mean that the couplet, as Molière uses it, must be a very supple form.

EH   Yes.

RW   I think it is. As he uses it, very often he will produce the equivalent of an aria. Then there will be the long speeches, recognizable as *tirades;* very often there will be stichomythia, the trading-off of couplets or of individual lines; then often there will be patterns in which people will exchange speeches of six lines in length. Very often when there is a six-line speech, it will break down into three couplets paralleling each other, repeating the thought in very much the way that the divisions of the sonnet often do. And, of course, many Molière plays break briefly into prose. A letter, for example, will be in prose.

EH   So you're pointing to the ways in which the standard couplet could be made various enough to accommodate certain changes.

RW   There are, additionally, songs and poems produced by the characters of the plays. M. Trissotin produces a horrible poem in *The Learned Ladies*.

EH   You chose to translate all four plays. You were not assigned to do them.

RW   No. I got the idea of doing *The Misanthrope* from having seen it done by the Comédie Française in 1948, and from having associations with The Poets Theatre in Cambridge, and from applying to the Guggenheims for an award which would enable me to write a poetic play. I did try to write one in New Mexico, but had no luck. It occurred to me that translating *The Misanthrope* would be a good thing to do in itself, and might teach me something about poetry in the theater. I don't think that I had any thoughts of performance when I started out. I was simply producing, I hoped, a finished reading version. And I was rather surprised, when The Poets Theatre did it in 1955, to find how satisfactorily it worked on the stage, since I had practically no experience in the theater and didn't know how to write for actors. I know that my later translations of Molière are better paced and articulated for the voices of actors and actresses than *The Misanthrope* is.

EH   So that after having stumbled on a way to make voices viable in translation, you found yourself listening to what you were doing with that consciousness, knowing that the work would be performed.

RW   Yes, as soon as The Poets Theatre started producing *The Misanthrope*—and then afterwards, when it was done in New York and began to be done in other places—I found myself hanging around the theater listening to people wrestling with what I'd written.

EH   And then discovering surprising things, no doubt.

RW   Yes, finding in some cases that I'd wrought better than I knew, and in some cases that I'd produced conjunctions of sounds that were difficult to articulate—or had, in choosing between two possible renderings of a line, taken the less dramatic way. Now I always say the lines aloud and imagine the thing in production.

EH   You think that has changed the way you write?

RW   Yes.

EH   So that in some ways you've become a dramatist despite yourself?

RW   Yes. And then, of course, all of this has had an effect upon my own poetry, which in a very general sense of the word has become more dramatic.

EH   The feeling you have about the writing of your own poetry is not a stable thing—it's modified all the time by the things you want to put into it, ways you want to get them into the poetry. And translation is an avenue that's always open in some way to provide you with certain alternatives to the ways you'd been writing before.

RW   Yes. It proves to be so. At the same time, as I've said, I'd never consciously use translation as a means to something else.

EH   Well, there's more to what one does than just producing something that works, isn't there? Some views of the translator and his product have it that all that counts is not any theory at all or even whether the translator knows the source language. All that matters is whether the translation works or not, and I have a feeling that's too blunt a view of what really is involved.

RW I couldn't possibly translate if I thought—what may well be true of one or two of my efforts—that the product was justified merely by its *working*. It has to work merely in a faithful way. There wouldn't otherwise seem to me to be any reason not to have written one's own poem, and there wouldn't seem to me any reason to put the name of the victimized author of the original to the translation.

EH I know you've written about this in an issue of *Translation* 2, the periodical published at Columbia, but I don't recall if you said anything about an aspect of the subject that I'd like to bring up now. Poets who have translated and then have themselves been subjected to translation by others must face a unique double process of transformation. I wonder if your feelings match those of other poets I've spoken to—that the translator should produce not a slavish imitation of the work but a readable poem in his or her own language, based on your work.

RW Well, I think there must come moments in the most faithfully intended translation when you have a choice between reproducing what is apparently, in the dictionary sense of the term, the exact meaning of the original, and falling below the aesthetic level of the rest, or providing what seems to you a close equivalent. I think that I would always go for the close equivalent in such a case. I like something that Jackson Mathews once said, when he was speaking well of my translation of *Tartuffe*. Instead of describing it as word-for-word faithful, he said that it was thought-for-thought faithful. Now if you propose to be thought-for-thought faithful, which means not leaving out any of the thoughts of the original, you can chuck particular words that don't have handsome equivalents in your own language.

EH It's clear that translation can never be word for word.

RW   Even when one is translating Molière, who really *is* close
to us. There are a lot of things in the English and American
traditions through which you can reach out to Molière, and you
can put him into a form that is oddly familiar to us, even though
rhymed drama isn't part of our recent tradition.

EH   How do you feel about translating from languages you
don't know, like Russian, Spanish, and Hungarian? I mean, if
you have a view that you must be more faithful than not to the
original text, then you must have to trust to the fact that your
informant in the language you don't know is faithful.

RW   Well, for one thing, I always get a lot of information out
of my informant. I spent, oh, a couple of days sitting and drink-
ing Scotch with Max Hayward while we talked over three poems
only of Voznesensky's. He read over the poems to me in Russian,
and he gave me, with admirable restraint, strictly prosaic trans-
lations of them, not pushing me toward one or another word
choice, and I asked him questions about the appropriateness of
the meters to the subject, and I asked questions about the in-
dividual Russian words—what their flavors were, whether they
were high or low—that sort of thing. I took notes all the time
about what he told me. By the time I was through, I really had
done about as much thinking (though not in the same order)
as I would do in producing a poem of my own. About as much
thinking, or researching, or recognizing, or questioning. I've just
translated two poems from Hungarian, using literal versions
sent me by the editors of the *New Hungarian Quarterly*, to
which were appended comments on the characters and tones
of the poems, and which were accompanied also by the origi-
nals. I would never try to translate anything without the original
there—even where I do not understand the language. Looking
at the originals of these Hungarian poems, I was able to catch

something of their rhythm. I recognized certain words, and so drew closer, or felt I was drawing closer, to the poems themselves. And I've done the same with Spanish. Of course, Spanish is not so forbidding a language, to someone who has French or Italian, as Hungarian would be. Yet I have asked an intolerable lot of questions of the people who were helping me with Spanish. In the case of Russian, I've boned up in a kind of elementary way on the language, so that at least I have leapt the hedge of the Cyrillic alphabet and can sound the lines to myself.

EH Do you get much from sound in Russian? Does it help in any way?

RW A good deal. And it helps me a good deal that I've heard many people declaim Russian poetry.

EH Do you think if English were declaimed, in the way that Russian conventionally is declaimed, that would similarly affect, let's say, some hypothetical translator of Poe?

RW It has to be Poe, doesn't it?

EH Well, maybe Vachel Lindsay would do.

RW Maybe Vachel Lindsay, Sidney Lanier's "Marshes of Glynn," maybe certain English poems. Some of Dowson or Yeats might do well if translated by someone accustomed to the declamatory.

EH I recall a reading where Voznesensky had worked up a way, which is very familiar now to his audiences here, of declaiming his poems, perhaps starting with a translation in English from a reader who accompanied him on the podium, then waving the translator aside at the last poem, and saying, "You aren't necessary now," and then speaking that poem about the bells so the sounds came through on their own in the best unadulterated Russian manner. Which brings up a question about the degree of one's knowledge of, or fluency in, a foreign language. If one knows, say, French well, it's not knowing it as well as any native knows it, even if he's bilingual, as Nabokov is, or Beckett, or Borges. What is so utterly familiar to him, especially if he's a writer, seems to channel itself into one place, which is what he can get out of it as a literary trove, rather than the idiom as it flows and flows ordinarily, when one is native to the language. I'm not sure this is clear. What I'm trying to say is that perhaps there isn't finally a knowledge of a language satisfactory enough to any translator so that he can always feel certain that he knows the right thing to know.

RW   I'm sure that's true. I rather suspect that if there's an exception to your rule it would be Nabokov.

EH   Perhaps so.

RW   I remember a sentence or so in a letter of Ezra Pound's to Iris Barry. He tells her that for purposes of translation, you don't have to know all those languages. You only have to know the words in the best poems in those languages. He's being preposterous, I think. He's probably aware of a certain bravado in what he's saying, and yet there's also a certain truth in it too. He's saying what it is you are in fact likely to be working with when you do a job of translation. I suppose for someone like Borges, who speaks a very easy English, the English of Robert Louis Stevenson is more central than it is for me, say. However good his English is, it's slightly odd—it's connected with, centered in, specific literary enjoyments of his past. My knowledge of any foreign language, even if I worked harder on it than I've ever done, would continue to be so limited it would still be much more literary than that of a native.

EH   One conclusion you could come to, then, about poets translating from a foreign language is that they are crafting a thing, an object, that becomes a poem, rather than using the language as a means of communication in the usual sense. The poet-translator is creating an object apparently that will stand in place, as say, in the original French, a poem of Baudelaire's does. The communication exists in terms of the object rather than a linguistic exchange inviting an immediate interpersonal response, as in a conversation.

RW   That's right. It's the making of an object rather than the getting of something off one's chest, or the addressing of a conjectural audience out there. I think I was confessing as much a few minutes ago when I said that when I translate I am putting such abilities as I have at the service of someone else's poem in another language. Now when I write a poem of my own, I don't think I'm putting my abilities at the service of anything—I don't think that way then. I think in a quite strictly Emersonian way about how a poem of my own comes about. What matters is what I'm saying and the form that the poem takes is simply a part of what I'm saying. If I approach a sonnet, for example of Borges, as I dared to do several times, I have to start with a consciousness that the sonnet form must be *coped* with. I do not *elect* it.

EH   As these things go, the realization is often surprising after one has done the work. Sometimes I wonder if one isn't translating all the time—even in writing one's own poems, in a sense. I don't mean in a general way, from experience and so on, but in using a language that's totally free flowing, the idiomatic English that one speaks as we're speaking it now . . .

RW   Yes.

EH   . . . suddenly becoming something else, transforming itself. . . .

RW   Yes, into something more condensed and precise.

EH   Yes.

RW   And then there's the translation from the preverbal. I happen to think, in the teeth of certain philosophers, that there are preverbal thoughts from which we fumblingly begin. Don't we often, well before the "idea" of a poem has begun to clarify, feel an odd certainty about the proportions of what is coming on, about its tenor, savor, stance, or mode—about the channels of logic or feeling in which it is going to run? I think of Yeats's statement that a poem often came to him first as a phrase of music. And there's a passage in Mallarmé somewhere that I may have misunderstood, but that comes to mind, in which the poet senses the awakening of a voice, perhaps his own, "Encore dans les plis jaunes de la pensée." I wonder if Aristotle, in deriving the formulae of the tragic and other emotions, may not have pointed in the direction of that speech-before-speech I'm talking about. I don't mean, for God's sake, that one makes an unconscious, abstract resolve to write a tragedy or a ballad—subject always comes first. What I mean is that the subject, before we fully know it, seems often to have done a good deal of occult marshaling.

When invited to choose and introduce a volume of Selected
Poems *for the 1978 edition of Witter Bynner's works, I ac-
cepted for two reasons. One was my wish to oblige my friend
Paul Horgan, who had known Bynner and who wanted me
to do the job. The other was my mistrust of reputation,
which made me curious to look into the work of one who
had been much lauded and was now obscure.*

Witter Bynner

YEATS PRAISED the "powerful, eloquent language" of Witter
Bynner's first volume, *An Ode to Harvard and Other Poems;*
E. A. Robinson said of *The New World* that he could not recall
any book "more thoroughly alive"; D. H. Lawrence found the
poems of *Caravan* "very sincere and really deep in life"; Allen
Tate was not alone in judging Bynner, as once he did, to be
"deservedly . . . a leading figure in American poetry." Neverthe-
less the editor of Louise Bogan's letters, published in 1973,
found it necessary to identify Witter Bynner in a footnote, say-
ing of him and of Arthur Davison Ficke that they "were poets
who, today, are best remembered as the perpetrators . . . of the
Spectra hoax." Best remembered, I fear, always means mostly
forgotten.

How to explain the forgottenness of a poet who was so val-
ued, in his day, by other poets whom we still read and esteem?
A simple answer might be that writers are often seen, in retro-
spect, to have overvalued their contemporaries, out of proximity
and a natural gratitude to all who are helping their moment to
find its voice. I think it no injustice to say that Bynner had not
the final stature of some who praised him. Yet he was and is a

true and valuable poet, as this book will prove, and it will not do to dismiss Yeats's words, or anyone else's, as puffery.

Leafing through the magazines in which Bynner published during the 1920's, one soon comes upon another answer to the question I have posed. In issues of *The New Republic*, for example, one repeatedly finds a whole page devoted to sonnets by several hands—by Elinor Wylie, Robert Hillyer, Sara Teasdale, Witter Bynner, and others. As it entered its second decade, the American poetic "renaissance," developing in many modes, had brought forward a corps of expert practitioners of the lyric, by which I here mean a shortish poem of personal feeling or perception, characterized at its best by intensity and by felicity of phrasing and form. Of all these admired and much-published lyricists, who were, to be sure, diverse within their apparent class, Edna Millay was the most Thespian and the most celebrated, and Bynner confidently declared her, in answer to a 1927 inquiry from *The Bookman*, to be the greatest living American poet. But a page in *The Nation* of June 9, 1926, indicates how things were going to go. At the bottom of the left-hand column is an agreeable and clever poem by Bynner in which, likening the repose of a quiet café, with its tables and tobacco smoke, to that of a desert tableland traversed by puffs of cloud, he prefers the remembered natural scene. In the right-hand column, however, is Mark Van Doren's review of *Selected Poems: 1909–1925*, by T. S. Eliot. The review acknowledges certain aspects of the expatriate Eliot which had caused early readers to resist him: his "difficulty," his aridity, his pessimism, his elegant weariness, "his indifference to most of the current poetic themes." But Van Doren also firmly states that Eliot is "one of the finest of twentieth century poets," that "literary historians five centuries hence may be able to sum up our generation" by quoting *The Waste Land*, and that many of his poems have already the character of classics. I do not pretend that there is anything crucial about this magazine page I have happened on, but it does represent one moment in an inexorable transition.

In his 1929 essay, *The Persistence of Poetry*, Bynner somewhat crankily said, "There are countless artificers, over-cultured and jaded, who with extensive knowledge of the world's poets and with the most highly self-conscious uses of prosody, fabricate words into strained and intellectualized meanings which pass for a season among the literary fashionables as poetry, but which are about as important to the singing heart of man as the latest sartorial trick from Paris." The only culprit specifically mentioned was Amy Lowell, and Bynner regarded her poetic and promotional career as faded; but he also warned against "a whole tribe of her nature" whose chieftain, I venture to guess, was that Eliot who would so largely dominate American poetry during the second quarter of this century. Bynner was right to fear what an Age of Eliot could and would do to that open sort of "song" which he most prized and was best equipped to write. If Dr. Williams felt that *The Waste Land*'s publication had blasted his enterprise—the articulation of America in its own word and cadence—he nonetheless survived the blast and went on to enjoy wide recognition and mentorship in the 1950's. And Hart Crane's *Bridge*, conceived as a visionary answer to Eliot's pessimism, went at once into the modern canon. As in any literary period, great things were achieved in spite of, or without reference to, those thought to be in the ascendancy. But the poetic practice of Eliot and others (the Fugitive group, for instance), and the related aesthetic of the New Criticism, fostered new tastes and standards in the light of which the well-turned passionate lyric of love, earth, death, and beauty seemed not to be doing the necessary job of art. Poetry must now, it was felt, cope with a complex time through a hard, intricate honesty of thought and emotion, a scope beyond the personal, a sophisticated cultural and historical awareness, a resolute inclusiveness in diction and matter, and a technique employing wit and irony in the service of precision. As that prescription more and more prevailed, the reputation of Millay began to wither, and other talents loosely comparable to hers—some of them finer than hers—were not encouraged to be productive. By 1938, Benét and Pearson could say in their *Oxford Anthology of American Literature*, "Witter Bynner is one of the few men writing poetry today in whose work may be found any considerable body of the simple lyric."

Good art, of whatever magnitude, is never replaced, but it may well be mislaid. It is writers, I think, who are most likely to be recklessly attached, regardless of critical orthodoxy and of their own practice, to poems not currently in vogue. I can think of one thoroughly "experimental" poet on whom Elinor Wylie has been a recent influence; of another given to reading aloud from Charlotte Mew; of another who has kept me up half the night with his total recall of Bynner's beloved Housman. And I have heard a playwright of unimpeachable contemporaneity say from memory an exquisite sonnet by Lizette Woodworth Reese. With anthologists, professors, and critics it is generally otherwise. E. C. Stedman's *American Anthology*, published in 1900, had room for everyone past or present, not excluding John Quincy Adams and Daniel Webster. But later anthologies of our national poetry have increasingly been intended not only for the window seat and bedside table but for the classroom desk. In response to the views and needs of professors, many anthologists have boiled down American poetry to the work of some fifty or sixty writers, all certifiably major. This work has in some cases been excellently done, and I make no objection to a stress upon what is best; but one may regret the presentation of poets *in vacuo*, the close decisions which have consigned fine talents to oblivion, and the inevitable bias against poetry which, in its forthrightness, would seem to leave a lecturer little to do. Among critical surveys of American verse, few recent studies approach the evocative fullness of David Perkins's *History of Modern Poetry*, which repeatedly restores a sense of the variety and precanonical incertitude of our literary past. It is far more usual to see a series of assured reputations revisited in the light of some notion of the "American experience" and of "main currents." I should guess that the surest way to have existed, in the eyes of most contemporary criticism, is to be discernible somewhere upon a line drawn through Emerson and Whitman.

Witter Bynner has not yet profited by that sort of tic-tac-toe, but in fact the strongest influence on his early thought, if not on his technique, was his fellow Brooklynite Whitman. *An Ode to Harvard* (1907) may seem to us, at least in its long title poem, an odd first book for a young man to have written. It had been one thing for Longfellow, in "Morituri Salutamus," to summon up a vanished Bowdoin at the fiftieth reunion of his class; it was another thing for Bynner, just five years out of college and embarked on an editorial career at *McClure's*, to return in homesick verse to Cambridge and the Yard, chasing memories of "goodies" and proctors, lamenting the old pump, and regretting high old times. We are helped to understand such a choice of subject if we recall Bliss Carman and Richard Hovey (author of the Maine "Stein Song"), who in the nineties had idealized athletic youth and comradeship, and if we remember that such colleges as Harvard, in the early 1900's, were seen not

only as educators of the *aristoi* but as instillers of moral and
spiritual purpose. Bynner's poem is thus able to move from nos-
talgia for his and Harvard's past to an affirmation of Harvard's
future and all mankind's, and to end by charging Harvard,
founded "for Christ and for His Church," to continue to bran-
dish "the spear of youth" in "the spirit's fight."

The best lines in the poem, those concerning Mount Auburn
Cemetery, were commended by A. E. Housman as "really beau-
tiful poetry," and are in their substance far more Whitmanian
than Christian: the soul's destiny, they assert, is more and more
to incorporate all other souls, through universal love, until

> *. . . all shall be the mother and the son,*
> *The daughter and the father and the one.*

The poem is not everywhere so elevated in its language; there
is a fair amount of "sincere" and exclamatory gush which would
have made Stephen Crane, for one, grit his teeth; there are also
passages which are colloquial or slangy to good effect, as when
a Yale-Harvard game is described in a boisterous style and
form strikingly anticipatory of Lindsay's "Bryan, Bryan, Bryan,
Bryan." Underlying both the bouncy and the vatic portions of
the poem, one senses a radical solitude akin to Whitman's, the
sort of solitude which might make one hanker for a fusion with
all humanity. The football game is seen as an event which "con-
gregates/ The many into one," and the memory of undergradu-
ate friendships causes Bynner to exclaim,

> *O blessed are the early ways to share*
> *The mystery of being not alone!*

It was not the gamey, exhibitionistic Whitman whom Bynner
followed, and continued to follow; nor was it the bold confronter

of pain, evil, and shame. The Whitman whom Bynner's next work acknowledges by name is the finished prophet of spiritual democracy, his visions calmed, codified, and—as Paul Horgan has put it—ultimately translated "into the terms of the Wilsonian *Zeitgeist.*" In Bynner's Phi Beta Kappa poem, "The Immigrant," given at Harvard in 1911 and later enlarged into *The New World* (1915), the poet speaks chiefly as a good student who is transmitting to us the wisdom of others. This student has for his teacher and inspirer a woman named Celia, and Bynner tells us in a note that Celia is a real woman, now dead, whom her poet has idealized, gathering "into her large spirit the beauties of many women, into her words the wisdom of many men, as stars into the one heaven." This haloed and educative spirit, this Egeria, has herself a beloved instructor in Walt Whitman, and thus the thought of Bynner's poem is doubly sanctioned, oracular in depth.

What does the poem reveal? Celia tells the poet that "the love of two," such as they enjoy, "incurs the love of multitudes," because each of us is a part of everyone else, and the flow of history is toward unselfish brotherhood and spiritual unity. This process is irresistible: "something pure and exquisite,/ Although inscrutably begun,/ Surely exalts the many into one." To "seek out the single spirit" by embracing all others is to "join God's growing mind," a mind which grows toward a final condition of divine wholeness, beauty, peace, and love. America has a special role in that evolution because, where democracy exists and social justice is an acknowledged goal, a man can most readily "know all men to be himself." As immigrant ships have sought America out of the dark past, and from every corner of the world, America is itself a figurative ship bound for an ideal "new world." Already, it and mankind are under way: economic

injustice is being overcome, the inclination toward war is yielding
to a "fellowship of unshed blood," and evil is ever more clearly
seen to be the "temporary pain" of giving birth to future good.

Where Whitman best persuades us, in his own work, is in
those poems which do not simply set forth a finished doctrine
but fight their way instead through sloughs and storms of the
mind toward a manic capacity to be "orotund, sweeping, and
final." In *Song of Myself*, Whitman's ideas are thus in a sense
validated—shown to be possible and achievable—by their visi-
ble emergence from one man's psychic struggle. The thought of
The New World has no such dramatic persuasiveness, and must
convince by its adequacy to life, by its internal coherence, and
by the rhetoric in which it is couched. I do not find the poem
altogether convincing, though there are fine rhetorical passages
like this, in which Celia is affirming the omega point:

> *It is my faith that God is our own dream*
> *Of perfect understanding of the soul.*
> *It is my passion that, alike through me*
> *And every member of eternity,*
> *The source of God is sending the same stream.*
> *It is my peace that when my life is whole,*
> *God's life shall be completed and supreme.*

Considered as a religious utterance, whether Christian or tran-
scendentalist, the poem leaves the reader uneasy. God as cre-
ator is minimized. It is not clear whether the God who impels
history is a mind or a mere force; if He is the latter, it is not
explained how a force could will itself to develop an encom-
passing mind. Christ the Lord is demoted to be Christ the com-
rade, "a man who proved man's unused worth—/ And made
himself the God"; and though the poem speaks often of im-

mortality or resurrection, and proclaims that "Nothing is lost," it appears on the whole that we shall survive death only as re-cycled matter and in the memories of those we have edified. If Bynner were, like Yeats, the poet of a "system," related works might iron out all questions and tell us to what genre of poem *The New World* truly belongs. Lacking such aids, I shall say that the poem is a fervent and naïve humanitarian exhortation, an appeal to social conscience which exploits both Walt Whitman and the author's felt but irregular Christian faith. It is a poem which could, I think, be converted without much tinkering into a high-minded sort of Marxist vision. It is also the poem of a lonely young man who, somehow diffident about particular love, wishes in this life to merge with everybody at once, and in death to escape from the "incompleteness" of personal identity into the whole.

The tone of *The New World* must be "mystical" and "serene," those being among Celia's qualities, and so it has less flexibility of voice than did *An Ode to Harvard*; but the two poems use the same quite loose form, their lines varying freely in length and rhyming according to no set scheme. The advantages of such a form might be a capacity for expressive dilation or con-traction, and an ease in the emphatic placement of important words. The danger of such a form is that it invites laziness, opportunistic rhyming, and the loss of rhythmic character for want of a norm. Housman, writing to Bynner about the poem in its first form, said, "The only criticism I have to make, if it is a criticism, is that my personal ear is not pleased by verses of more than 10 syllables in this mixed metre, though I know that Patmore and others have used them." Anyone's ear, I should think, would have trouble with lines like "As with wonder at an unseen figure carrying a grail," or "And then of a sudden she had run forth from her hiding-place." *The New World* is not a sustained performance, whether in technique or in its rather static argument, but it may be mined for handsomely turned passages such as the one here printed as "Grieve Not for Beauty."

The mature Bynner, whom we begin to meet in *Grenstone Poems* (1917), would probably not dissent from what I have just said: the passage which I have mentioned was salvaged as a self-sufficient poem in his *Selected Poems* (1936), and again in the later *Book of Lyrics* (1955); and Bynner was to essay the long poem once more only, in *Eden Tree*. I have dwelt at some length on his first extended efforts because, for all its shifts and phases, Bynner's later poetry was remarkably continuous with his first preoccupations; but from now on he was to be, in theory and in practice, a lyric poet. Only such a poet would describe a master as one "who can so use language that a whole vast sky of words seems as simple as a petal." Only such a poet would find in Housman's verse "all the great machinery of Greek purgation gathered into a dewdrop." In casual answer to a letter asking him why he wrote poetry, Bynner once replied, "The best I can say is that I still feel as I felt from boyhood, that there is importance in trying to condense a whole novel, say, or a whole symphony into a few pages or even eight lines. . . . I know that epics hold an important place in literary history, but I venture to point out the fact that they are in the long run mainly memorable because of imbedded lyrics." Whether advanced by Bynner or by the Poe whom he early cherished, such claims for the lyric, though they indicate a truth, are obviously disputable. Any art form which works has need of all its means. The wrath of Achilles really does take twenty-odd books to tell, and the machinery of purgation, in *Oedipus Rex*, will not turn without all the parts discerned by Aristotle. An eight-line lyric might "say the same thing," but not to the same effect. A stanza or two might argue, as Bynner so often did, the responsibility of each for all, but when that idea transpires from the many concretely interwoven lives of *The Brothers Karamazov*, the mode of proof and the nature of the impact are different. Let it be enough to say of the lyric that it can be language at its most compressed, that it can give the suddenest of immortal wounds, and that it is rightly likened, at times, to the dropped pebble which causes widening circles in water.

Grenstone Poems was on the whole a gathering of short poems from the decade following 1907, the year in which Bynner decided against an editorial career and retired to write in Cornish, New Hampshire. Cornish is "Grenstone," and Grenstone is Bynner's Shropshire: there are, as might be expected, a few poems reminiscent of Housman—verses written in homesick absence from the countryside, stanzas which speak of "lads," runners, and so on. But actually the volume is extremely diverse in tenor and mode: there are experiments in strict or relaxed *vers libre*, incantatory poems of the sort that Lindsay was doing, a long Sandburgian paragraph-poem, songs, ballads, epigrams, and even a doggerel piece in Negro dialect. Thematically, *Grenstone Poems* has a certain amount of cohesion through its many poems of Celia—of the poet's love for her, of her death and ideal continuance, of the spirit of all-embracing love which she inculcates and symbolizes. In this book of consistently wide sympathies, whose poet declares, "For I am nothing if I am not all," the mockingbird is characteristically praised because in him "all birds" are joined in the one medley, and there must even be a poem for Kansas, in which the poet, though a devotee of New Hampshire hills, reassures the prairie of his affection for its "easy ample flow."

Bynner always wished his books to be unities, rather than mere accumulations. He best realized this wish in such a book as *Indian Earth*, where a new subject matter and a fresh aesthetic discover their appropriate and sustainable form. We have the impulse at its most trivial in *Book of Lyrics*, where poems selected from many earlier books are sorted according to the four seasons. A poet of Bynner's lyric temper is always in danger of tidiness, a tidiness which will smother the incipient poem in a neat stanza pattern full of graceful phrases and hill-rill rhymes. I think that I discover such a tidying urge in the too-elaborate organization of *Grenstone Poems*, which is divided into three titled sections, each divided in turn into many subsections having titles and two-line mottoes. It is hard for me to see why this interesting poem, called "Driftwood," should have been assigned to subsection IV ("Dalliance") of Section I ("Grenstone"):

> *Come, warm your hands*
> *From the cold wind of time.*
> *I have built here, under the moon,*
> *A many-colored fire*
> *With fragments of wood*
> *That have been part of a tree*
> *And part of a ship.*
>
> *Were leaves more real,*
> *Or driven nails,*
> *Or fingers of builders,*
> *Than these burning violets?*
> *Come, warm your hands*
> *From the cold wind of time.*
> *There's a fire under the moon.*

That is a disciplined free-verse poem, varying narrowly between lines of two or three stresses, and disposed in two paragraphs of seven lines each. It is about a fire made of driftwood on a chill, gusty, and moonlit beach, and the poet invites us to share it. The words never forsake their literal subject, and continually render the scene more vivid to the eye: driftwood does in fact burn with many colors, and through the mention of leaves, nails, shipbuilders' fingers, and violets we imagine the several shapes and behaviors of the flames. But of course the cold wind of the second line is not merely a wind: it is also "time." The poet invites us to meditate, in the presence of a driftwood fire, on that time which coldly destroys all things, bringing down the tallest tree and wrecking the best-made vessel. We are asked whether the tree and the ship were "more real" than their now burning fragments, and it is assumed that we know the answer. I should say that Bynner is here doing a dangerous and delicate thing, since it would be so possible to construe the whole poem as an invitation to take refuge from a sense of temporal loss in Buddha's teaching that all things are illusory and "on fire." But even if *Grenstone Poems* did not begin with a poem ("This Wave") which says "What was ended/ Has begun," and end with the poet moving forward and upward on a Whitmanian spiritual journey, I think that "Driftwood" would be sufficiently weighted toward another interpretation. The fire, as Bynner describes it, is not simply the annihilation of wood fragments; even as the wrecked ship of the poem was built of felled trees, the fire is something "built" of ship's driftwood by the poet's hands and offered us as a warming symbolic proof that time is not a destroyer but a perpetual renewer. Out of all change comes new life, as in the variously colored violets of spring; we are to warm our hands at flames in which we see the fingers of dead builders, and then turn to fresh work; and the moon, above such a fire, is a light which forever rises and waxes again.

This brief, plain-seeming, subtle poem, in which all the words prove to be working hard, and in which the meaning seems to emerge uncoerced from the data, is for my taste more compelling than *The New World*'s grandiloquent assertions that "Nothing is lost," and points toward the best qualities of Bynner's later achievements.

Robert Hunt, who edited the *Selected Poems* of 1936, was quite right to place *Spectra* (1916) after *Grenstone Poems* (1917); the *Spectra* poems came after most of *Grenstone* in date of composition, and represent an inadvertent modulation toward Bynner's next serious work, *The Beloved Stranger*. As everyone more or less knows, *Spectra* was a hoax cooked up by Bynner (under the name of Emanuel Morgan) and Arthur Davison Ficke (as Anne Knish). Its intention was to make fun, by seemingly serious precept and example, of schools of poetry and their apologists, and in particular of Imagism, Vorticism, and Futurism. Anne Knish's preface (which was, of necessity, collaborative) is a highly plausible bit of pomposity, no sillier on the face of it than most other manifestoes. It defines "Spectric" composition as the poet's breaking up of "the white light of infinite existence" into delectable colors, as the imitation of the eye's and the spirit's afterimages, and as the presentation not only of the object but of its "spectres"—the shadowy and sometimes grotesque ideas which, in the poet's imagination, surround the object and are its true essence. It will be seen that the Spectric program recommends a wild subjectivity in the collocation of images, intended perhaps to burlesque the theory behind such brusque juxtapositions as we find in Pound's famous "In a Station of the Metro"; it also proposes to outdo, in lavish color imagery, the more visual of the Imagists, against whose precious jasmines and alizarins Williams had protested in "To a Solitary Disciple."

The preface further prescribes "a tinge of humor," albeit with a mock-serious purpose—to support the poet's "intuition of the Absolute" by a stress on the vanity of lowly man. The fact that humor was an acknowledged seasoning in the Spectric recipe may to a slight extent excuse the gullibility with which *Spectra* was received by distinguished critics, distinguished poets, and the public. Still, it is hard for us to conceive of anyone's perusing with *any* sobriety Emanuel Morgan's "Opus 104," which begins

> *How terrible to entertain a lunatic!*
> *To keep his earnestness from coming close!*

—let alone "Opus 14," which closes with the outrageous lines

> *Then you came—like a scream*
> *Of beeves.*

In any case, as William Jay Smith has told in *The Spectra Hoax*, all manner of people were taken in, and the spoof was long undetected. It went to show what has often been evidenced in later decades, that when people are aflutter about schools and ideologies of art, their perceptions of particular art works are likely to be unwary and obtuse.

Bynner's own later comment, it is reported, was that Emanuel Morgan had been less of a joke on the critics who took him seriously than on Bynner himself, who took him for a joke. When a poet turns to nonsense or travesty or satire, his poems, in addition to accomplishing their primary aim, will often embody or liberate some aspect of himself. "Opus 79," for all its foolishness, seems to conclude on a familiar note of Whitmanian ubiquity, and "Opus 78" ("I am beset by liking so many people") is Bynner's old theme of universal love restated with a Spectric extravagance and a certain exasperation. As for liberations, one reason why Ficke and Bynner could hide for so long behind their pseudonyms was that nothing like *Spectra* was expected of them. Ficke had worked in sonnet sequences and formal lyrics; Bynner had, to be sure, written all sorts of poems, including little free-verse amusements like this, which appeared in a 1915 issue of *The Smart Set*:

> *Passion transforms me from my puny build . . .*
> *Your bosom listens to me like a crowded balcony*
> *To a great man speaking.*

But prior to *Spectra* he was to the public, and to himself, the high-minded author of *The New World* and of the forthcoming *Grenstone Poems*. The experience of collaborating on a parodic hoax seems to have loosened his bondage to an effusive idealism and an endearing persona; he might now, when the subject matter warranted, feel freer to be sharp, witty, intuitive, or outlandish.

The *Beloved Stranger* (1919) was serially published in *Reedy's Mirror* as "Songs of the Unknown Lover," the first installments appearing anonymously and the latter ones being credited to Bynner. The poems were, however, the work of Bynner's *Doppelgänger* Emanuel Morgan, as Bynner had quite seriously confessed in a letter to Thomas Raymond. Several of *The Beloved Stranger*'s less elevated poems were revisions of earlier Spectric pieces; nevertheless, the book is a unified and serious work, having no element of hoax in it, and my guess is that Bynner wrote it "as by Emanuel Morgan" because the temporary disguise emboldened him to depart from his previous norms of thought, expression, and technique. Also, perhaps—though I cannot give hard proof of this—because the book arose from a critical emotional experience calling for some measure of camouflage.

In Bynner's earlier poems, God is less a transcendent being than a fullness which the poet, and mankind, are in process of achieving through human brotherhood. Thus the last lines of *Grenstone* read:

> *I have been waiting long enough ...*
> *Impossible gods, good-by!*
> *I wait no more ... The way is rough—*
> *But the god who climbs is I.*

The poems of *The Beloved Stranger* are not in that key at all. They are mysterious, ambiguous, and cannot be neatly expounded, but the divinity to whom they are addressed—though once described by the poet as "a part of my soul passing and I not finding it"—is high, secret, timeless, and absolute. Utterly un-Whitmanian, and superior to "common things," he is shadowed forth in sun, sky, lightning, and sea, and may sometimes be approached in dream. Himself not transitory, he is periodically embodied in the poet's transitory lovers. Of these we glimpse but little—a hand here, a shoulder there—and they are chiefly felt as occasions of rapturous communion with the god. When we hear of a cascade of hair, or the snow valley of a breast, we envision less the human lover than the natural beauty which is the god's symbolic vestment. Despite its moments of rapture, *The Beloved Stranger* is a painful book concerned with the emotional predicaments of ideal love: human attachment does not always conduce to vision and joy; it can be degrading, and it passes; the unknown divinity, who is inaccessible to language or reason, cruelly absents himself, and yet the thought of him devalues the actual.

> *How is it,*
> *That you, whom I can never know,*
> *My beloved,*
> *Are a wall between me and those I have known well—*
> *So that my familiars vanish*
> *Farther than the blue roofs of Nankow*
> *And are lost among the desert hills?*

In general, the movement of the book is from happiness to spiritual and erotic loss, thence to a sardonic repudiation of human love—

> *The look in your eyes*
> *Was as soft as the underside of soap in a soap-dish . . .*

> *And I left before you could love me.*

—and finally to a renewed acceptance both of the poet's lovers and of his ideal Beloved, together with all of the bitter contradictions involved.

Whitman's ebullient and godlike incorporation of all life, in *Song of Myself*, yielded to a darker mood in "Out of the Cradle Endlessly Rocking," where he became the poet of lost love and of death. Scholars have attributed the shattering of Whitman's narcissism, which was the emotional basis of the first poem, to a belated and unhappy love affair with a particular person; I dare assume—to return to my earlier conjecture—that *The Beloved Stranger* testifies to a like development in Bynner's emotional life, which was, as I have noted, centrally solitary, and was further complicated by bisexuality. Babette Deutsch, reviewing the book in *The Dial*, discerningly described its songs as "the outcry of that profound solitude which the plummet of love itself begins to sound," and added that the Stranger, whether lost lover or unknown god, "is one who gives . . . the perfection of withheld things." The new perspectives of *The Beloved Stranger* are almost certainly to be accounted for in personal terms, and not merely, though some have thought so, as the result of Bynner's first visit to the Orient in 1916. The Orient is, to be sure, conspicuously present in the properties of the poems: in the roofs of Nankow, in temples, in cherry blossoms, in jade. And if the poems' free forms and surprising images are a strange legacy from *Spectra*, one must agree with W. M. Reedy that they have also a spare suggestiveness arguing a familiarity with *haiku* and *tanka*. However prompted and however influenced, the best poems of *The Beloved Stranger* are among the best poems of Witter Bynner, having, for all their mystery and indirection, a clean accuracy of feeling.

China was to have a great effect on the remainder of Bynner's career. In 1918, while engaged in a year's teaching of public speaking and verse writing at Berkeley, he met the scholar Kiang Kang-hu, with whose aid he undertook the translation of a T'ang anthology. After a decade's devoted labor, this came out in 1929 as *The Jade Mountain*. Meanwhile, there were *Pins for Wings* (1921), a little book of free-verse impressions of fellow writers, and two collections of lyrics, *A Canticle of Pan* (1920) and *Caravan* (1925). The latter two abandon the vein of *The Beloved Stranger*, revert in good part to the forms of *Grenstone*, and are, for all their thematic groupings, quite miscellaneous. Still, there are constants to be noted. If the poet of *A Canticle of Pan* no longer lays down the Whitmanian gospel, and makes no claims to godhead, the collection is nonetheless permeated, through good poems and bad, by that outreaching spirit which Bynner always had: Pan and Christ and Buddha are all to be embraced and reconciled; the lives of Chinese and of Russians are to be entered and warmly understood; there is compassion for every victim, reproof for all that is cold and exclusive, and abhorrence of the wars which embitter and divide mankind. When any of this is stridently noble, or simplistically fervent, it fails; Bynner would never cease to write poems of protest, exhortation, and argument, but where he is most successful is in lines which seem to come not from a speaker who is marshaling his thoughts and images but from a man who notices, responds, and records. Here, in the poem "Meadow-Shoes," is a curious and minor instance of noticing:

> My shoe-soles, wet in the meadow,
> Sang like the chirrup of birds—
> But like birds of only a note or two,
> Like persons of few words.
>
> And, O my shoes, how hard it is
> To tell the joy you touch!
> I know, for I have tried to sing
> The things I love too much.

A speaker-poet would never in ten thousand lines say anything about the musical limitations of wet shoe soles; but the recorder-poet, the poet to whom things occur, is responsive to reality's neglected trifles. The movement of thought here, from shoe squeak to bird song to poetry, is odd but plausible enough; it is not like Bryant's occasional wrenching of a moral from some woodland creature; but Bynner is aware of passing from a small, little-mentioned thing to a larger notion, and so disarms us with the comic inflation of "O my shoes."

A weightier piece of recording, and one which gains force with each rereading, is "In Kamakura."

> *In Kamakura, near the great Diabutsu,*
> *When I had sat a long time on the ground*
> *And been gathered up, forgetful of my face and form,*
> *Into the face and form of endless dream,*
> *I found among the booths a little pendant Buddha*
> *With the steel of a round mirror for His halo . . .*
>
> *So that a brooding head still intervenes in bronze*
> *Between my face and the image of my face,*
> *And I cannot see myself and not see Him.*

This is a poem both narrative and descriptive, which imparts an extraordinary amount in nine effortless and transparent lines. The scene is simply set; we are given the poet's meditative state to prepare us for the impact of the little Buddha which he purchases; and then the Buddha, and the act of looking at him, are so presented as to objectify a profoundly inward experience—a Westerner's encounter with the Buddhist release from self. A further virtue of the poem lies in its rhythm; Bynner has, by mid-line pauses, rhythmic variations, and hypermetrical lines, prevented his single sentence from marching through the pentameter in a manner inappropriate to the subject. If the words of the poem deftly externalize a spiritual event, its movement has the hovering progress of memory and thought.

Some of the brief characterizations of *Pins for Wings* (as when George Santayana is defined as "a withered/ rose-window," or W. C. Williams as "carbolic acid/ in love") foreshadow what is most notable in *Caravan*. Bynner's poetic voice, when first heard, had been a warm and generous one— and one gathers that warmth and generosity were at all times real qualities of the man. (He was, for one thing, a lifelong encourager of younger artists; my own sole communication with him, if I may offer a bit of parenthetical witness, came when one of my first publications, in *The Harvard Advocate*, brought a kind note of approval from his desk in Santa Fe.) But poetry is most credible when it seems to bear the impress of a whole personality, warts and all; and so it is good to be fully assured, in *Caravan*, that Bynner's voice can have an edge to it. The gift for acerbity which had briefly surfaced in *Spectra* and *The Beloved Stranger* is now displayed at leisure in an attack on his friend D. H. Lawrence, who had visited Mexico with Bynner and was soon to portray him unflatteringly in *The Plumed Serpent*. "D. H. Lawrence" is a derisive portrait of a cat-man or man-cat who hates civilized humanity and fancies himself as a savage spirit attuned to the "life-urge" of the cosmos.

> *Do you see that the moon is on its back for you?*
> *And has turned up the white fur of its belly*
> *And put out a silver-haired paw?*

Bynner himself had once felt identified with cosmic processes, but of a more upward-tending and cheerful kind; Lawrence's dark primitivism, and its consequences for human relations, he could not stomach. There are three reasons, I should suppose, why Lawrence could forgive the poem and praise the volume in which it appeared. In the first place, it is a strong, resourceful, witty invective, worthy of its subject. In the second place, it is unanswerably accurate as to Lawrence's weaknesses and inner divisions. In the third place, it does Lawrence the honor of denouncing the cat-man in just such urgently iterative *vers libre* paragraphs as Lawrence had devoted to bats and snakes in *Birds, Beasts and Flowers* (1923).

There are other pieces in *Caravan* which represent new developments of tone, new unfoldings of personality. There is the muted astringency of "A Country Cottage," and in "Donald Evans," with its splendid use of the word "decorate," Bynner employs a dry and Latin-rooted pathos suggestive of Robinson. Here and there in *Caravan* are references to mesas, to San Felipe, to Chapala, reminding us that Bynner had now settled for good in Santa Fe—traveling often into old Mexico—and that his new territory and his continuing study of Chinese poetry would soon converge in his mind to produce what may be his most satisfying book of verse.

In *The Persistence of Poetry* (1929), which incorporated his introduction to *The Jade Mountain*, Bynner makes plain the conceptions of poetry, and of Chinese poetry in particular, which resulted in the Chapala section of *Indian Earth*. Poetry everywhere began, he tells us, by issuing, together with music, from "the heart and lips of simple mankind." Satiated and fatigued by culture, we Westerners have come to be "intellectually estranged from the simple sources of poetry." Why, then, has poetry so vitally persisted in China, where "centuries ago, cultured Chinese had reached the point of intellectual saturation which has tired the mind of the modern European"? Why do the street cries and rock inscriptions of China attest to the fact that poetry has never ceased, for the Chinese, to be "a natural and solacing part of life"? Bynner takes his answer from the scholar Ku Hung-ming, who in his pamphlet *The Spirit of the Chinese People* attributes China's eternal youth to "the fact that the average Chinese has managed to maintain within himself the head of a man and the heart of a child."

The exceedingly difficult technical rules of T'ang verse,

which govern the number of characters, the number of lines, the pattern of tones, the required grammatical parallelism, the placement and nature of rhymes, and the avoidance of repeated characters, had no interest for Bynner as translator or poet. "The discovery," he said,

> which has largely undone my early convictions as to the way of writing poetry has really to do with use of substance.... Mencius said long ago, in reference to the Odes collected by Confucius: "Those who explain the Odes must not insist on one term so as to do violence to a sentence, nor on a sentence so as to do violence to the general scope. They must try with their thoughts to meet that scope, and then they will apprehend it." In the poetry of the west we are accustomed to let our appreciative minds accept with joy this or that passage in a poem—to prefer the occasional glitter of a jewel to the straight light of the sun. The Chinese poet seldom lets any portion of what he is saying unbalance the entirety. Moreover... Chinese poetry rarely trespasses beyond the bounds of actuality. Whereas western poets will take actualities as points of departure for exaggeration or fantasy or else as shadows of contrast against dreams of unreality, the great Chinese poets accept the world exactly as they find it in all its terms, and with profound simplicity find therein sufficient solace. Even in phraseology they seldom talk about one thing in terms of another, but are able enough and sure enough as artists to make the ultimately exact terms become the beautiful terms. If a metaphor is used, it is a metaphor directly relating to the theme, not something borrowed from the ends of the earth. The metaphor must be concurrent with the action or flow of the poem; not merely superinduced, but an integral part of both the scene and the emotion.

Here, from *The Jade Mountain*, is Bynner's Englishing of Li Po's eight-line *shih* poem, "A Farewell to a Friend."

> *With a blue line of mountains north of the wall,*
> *And east of the city a white curve of water,*
> *Here you must leave me and drift away*
> *Like a loosened water-plant hundreds of miles...*
> *I shall think of you in a floating cloud;*
> *So in the sunset think of me.*
> *...We wave our hands to say good-bye,*
> *And my horse is neighing again and again.*

This exemplary translation illustrates everything which Bynner found attractive and corrective in Chinese poetry. Everything is distributed, in these quiet lines, with an evenness of attention; there is nothing of what Yeats called "insubordination of detail," and there are no ostentatious felicities of language. Everything in the scene and situation is actual, and presented in a natural sequence. The figures of speech involve no violent amalgamations: that is, if one's friend is going on a river journey, it is reasonable to think of a loosened water plant; that done, since the poem occurs under the open sky, it is not hard to associate the traveler with a floating cloud as well, and the poet's sinking heart with the sunset. The horse in the last line is neighing for equine reasons, but I suspect that we are to be reminded of the sounds of human grief. What no single good translation can convey to us is the cumulative force, in such poetry as Li Po's, of great images of the natural world. I do not know whether, in the above farewell poem, the mountain and river of the first two lines are to be felt as juxtaposed symbols of staying and going; but it is certain that all such imagery, in its beauty and permanence, is a consoling background to that melancholy, loneliness, or trouble usually present in the human dimension of T'ang poetry.

Bynner found, in Santa Fe and Chapala, physical resemblances to Peking, and in the Indians of New and old Mexico he saw the heirs of a majestic and ultimately Asiatic culture, still gifted with song and at one with the earth. In the Chapala section of *Indian Earth* he therefore presented, through eight-line *shih* poems, the Mexican Indian in a Chinese key. All of this, though nowhere insistently argued, is quite explicit. The musicians of Chapala are attuned to the mountains and the lake waves; the sensibility of a blind guitarist belongs "centuries back in Asia"; Bynner wishes to concenter the world on observed detail as with "the point of a brush in ancient Chinese fingers"; one of his lines in "Crow's Feet" is an echo of Li Po, and there is a whole poem ("Tulé") about loosened water plants. Buying in the market a brightly painted dish or other "toy," he observes that "Unless we remain children, we grow too old"—a sentiment which recalls Ku Hung-ming's words on the perpetual youthfulness of China. Finally, sun, moon, lake, and mountain afford, in Chapala as in China, a constant resource for the heart troubled by ephemeral human things:

> *. . . even the look of a well-beloved child*
> *Is lesser solace than a mountain-rim.*

The Chapala poems are, as the reader will see, a remarkably successful experiment. I need not recite their virtues, because they are precisely those which Bynner had found important in the poetry of China and had specified in *The Persistence of Poetry*. Fortunately, he proved able to embody them not only in translations but in original English verse. On the whole, his Mexican octaves are blither in mood than the T'ang poems on which they are modeled, and the reason for that is not far to seek. *Indian Earth* is a volume in which the lyric ego and its moods or troubles are not central: the poet's attention is turned outward, in an effort to evoke a culture which delights and moves him, and he does so in a modest and objective style, losing himself, as never before, in the lives of an ancient people. There may be moments of travel writing in the book, or touches of anthropology, but above all it is an act of happy communion. Hildegarde Flanner, discussing the Mexican poems, rightly connects them with Bynner's "early desire for fellowship," and observes that *Indian Earth* "comes close to the reality of union and compassionate brotherhood" in a way that *The New World*, with its abstract and theoretical benevolence, could not.

And yet, of course, Bynner was as much a "foreigner" in Chapala as he declared Lawrence to be in the poem so titled; he was not a Mexican Indian but a rich, serape-buying, party-giving visitor from "that northern country overrun with gringos." If *Indian Earth* is a sensitive and loving expression of a place and its people, if Bynner could lose himself for a while in writing of Chapala, that self was still, at fifty, somewhat troubled and unfound. And so it is not wholly strange to see him abruptly turning from the outwardness and relative self-effacement of *Indian Earth* to *Eden Tree* (1931), a book-length inquiry into his own history and nature.

Bynner thought of *Eden Tree* as a sequel to *The New World*. There are various ways of understanding that. For one thing, we have once again a long poem done in mixed meters and irregular rhyme—a form now handled more adroitly, and with an occasional brilliance. More significant, we have another poem rooted in Whitman, and Douglas Day is right to characterize it as "a sort of *Song of Myself* in modern dress." It is also a sequel in a special palinodial sense, because the hope of escaping isolation through universal love is now set aside, and what the poem amounts to is a solitary soul's rehearsal of its wavering progress toward an acceptance of aloneness and self-dependency. In part, the poet sees himself as Everyman, and accordingly we have a mythic cast of characters in which the main figures are Adam (the poet), Eve (the poet's attraction to the wifely, the generative, the good), and Lilith (his attraction to lust, to freedom, to intoxications of body and spirit). There are also Confucius, Buddha, and Jesus, appearing in one aspect as philosophic or religious alternatives through which Everyman might find himself. But the poem is also the confession of a particular man, with his own peculiar history and emotional constitution, and therefore there is another set of characters, drawn from Bynner's life, who interlace with the mythic figures and overlap them, and are encountered on the plane of remembered personal experience. It is on this plane that the poem truly proceeds, in a narrative-dramatic form—not as a philosophical pilgrimage, but as a series of emotional reactions to persons, places, and vicissitudes. It begins with the poet taking leave of the dead Celia, who is the Eve-principle at its most positive, and of the fictive Celia, whose ventriloquial gospel can no longer suffice him. Setting forth unsponsored in quest of himself, he encounters Paul, "a flower/ Of isolate boyhood," a restless and handsome young man who becomes his "god" (and the god or lover of *The Beloved Stranger* poems, I should think). With Paul's early death, Bynner-Adam seeks ease in travel, imbibing something of Buddhism from an old Chinese priest, and communing on T'ai-shan with the spirit of Confucius, who recommends the life of reason and mocks the hope of "paradise apart from earth." These experiences proving "not enough,"

Adam succumbs in Shanghai, Peking, and later in New York to Lilith—that is, to debauchery with women, meanwhile suffering flashes of grief for Celia or Paul, and at one juncture feeling drawn into St. Patrick's, only to conclude that

> *not by this gallows-tree*
> *Is there respite for me.*

The action or drift continues, with Adam visiting the dinner tables of well-bred people and recoiling from their stuffiness toward Lilith again; recoiling then from Lilith and "Babylon" and seeking the mountains, where he feels for a time at one with the elements, "safe from men," and at peace with the ghosts of Paul and Celia; eschewing a return to Eve under the form of a tame and passionless marriage; reverting to "wild-fire" and "the crackle of lust" in the shape of another Lilith; proceeding by way of disgust to solitary drinking and homosexuality; and hoping, as a last resort, for the revival of certain old friendships, only to find that his friends have been so deformed by marriage and money-getting that they can no longer meet him freely "mind to mind."

This brings the poem to its crisis, and the resolution which follows is strongly reminiscent in pattern of the final movement of *Song of Myself*—especially of its sections 38, 41, and 52. Friendless and despairing, the poet remembers his old faith in the crucified and resurrected Christ, and takes heart; what revives him, however, is not Christ's doctrine or "dream" but His courage in living out His dream "alone." Thus fortified by example, Adam befriends his own suffering, exchanges loneliness for a strong aloneness, and feels expansive and free: he is no longer a crucified man but "Jove, with the wind in his vast beard/ Making music," Apollo with his lyre, Orpheus,

"Prometheus with his singing fire," and "even Buddha, set be-yond desire." Wishing "no mistress now, no Lord, no wife,/ But only himself and the wideness of the world," standing "apart from thought, from years," he is bravely alone with the enduring universe. At the close of the poem he plunges into a lake at dawn and merges, Whitman-fashion, with the elements of water and air. Losing his loneliness and his "own shape," he becomes "a man made new" and will "never be dead."

Richard Blackmur, reviewing *Eden Tree* in *Poetry* for January 1932, observed: "If there is a philosophic attitude gov-erning the poem, it is the double attitude of dramatic solipsism with regard to the human world combined with a kind of in-stinctive pantheism regarding the material world." That is wholly correct, and excellently said. As for solipsism, Bynner's Adam puts it plainly enough to himself:

> *It is Adam whom you condemn or praise*
> *And not these other persons, in images of yourself...*

What we examine in the poem is not other people, or the thoughts and faiths of mankind, but the inability of any of these to release the self-absorbed hero from his solitude and to pro-vide him with wholeness and social identity. There are many ways, as we have glimpsed, in which *Eden Tree* resembles *Song of Myself*, and one might add that the two poems are alike in developing less by argument than by "mood swings" or oscilla-tions of feeling; but more than a difference in quality makes them dissimilar. There is, no doubt, a level of analysis at which Bynner's solipsism and Whitman's incorporation of all life would seem paradoxically akin; but if we take seriously what the two poets say they are saying, Bynner's Adam is a "single, sep-arate person" in a sense which Whitman would think impoverished. It seems to me that the end of *Eden Tree*, for all its suggestion of Whitman's translation into grass and air, is not so much Whitmanian as it is an intensification of the conventional Chinese contrast between the often-rueful human realm and the serenity of nature. Turning wholly away from human and doctrinal entanglements, and accompanied only by his poetic gift, lone Adam entrusts himself to the mountains and the waters.

The *Selected Poems* (1936) reprinted a slightly revised *Eden Tree* in full; it is too long, in proportion to its merit, to be so treated in this volume, and I have found it hard to do the poem justice through excerpts. Unquestionably, I have done an injustice by subjecting it to summary, which can make any work whatever sound dismal or silly; but I saw no other way to trace Bynner's altering sense of things or to convey the nature of so curious a poem. There are a number of effective and courageously honest passages in *Eden Tree*, and its adaptability of tone, as Adam fluctuates between the squalid and the exalted, is often admirable. Of its weaknesses, let me mention two. As Blackmur implicitly complains, a poem which presents its hero with philosophical and religious challenges should not be written, as *Eden Tree* is, almost wholly on the level of emotional logic and temperamental reaction. Second, Bynner's identification with Adam or Everyman is partially valid (we all know Eve and Lilith and loneliness) and partially an imposture: for example, the voice which scorns "wiving" and working and rearing children as a craven surrender of one's mind and freedom is not the voice of Everyman but of a moneyed bohemian who, though he once proposed marriage to Edna Millay, was more strongly attracted to men than to women.

The anti-marriage theme is more amiably and acceptably

handled in several of the sonnets of *Guest Book* (1935), a series of portraits—harsh, malicious, ironic, compassionate, or admiring—which, in view of the conclusion of *Eden Tree*, sound downright gregarious. If any influence is felt in these poems it would be that of Robinson's sonnet portraits and sonnet narratives, especially in lines like these—

> *And to relieve him largely of the stuff*
> *That works in little cells behind the ear,*

which have a Robinsonian circumlocution and convolution.

Such a poem as "Benedick" exhibits both a similarity to Robinson and a lot of crucial differences.

> *His was a life of single blessedness,*
> *Doubled upon occasion but not often,—*
> *Because he still believed that toil can bless*
> *While toils can only enervate and soften.*
> *Therefore when twilight touched his studio*
> *With loneliness, he would relieve his labour*
> *By summoning his dog, and both would go*
> *To while away a while upon a neighbour . . .*
> *What happened to this bachelor of parts*
> *Not one of all his neighbours can explain.*
> *Had he a heart, then, like most other hearts?*
> *Had he found solitude only a vain*
> *Evasion, that his name is also hers*
> *And the hangings in his house are diapers?*

What mostly makes one think of Robinson, here, is the stated uncertainty of the poet and his neighbors as to the bachelor painter's motive for marrying. Robinson's Tilbury Town is full of hearts which no one can quite fathom, and indeed the shal-

lowness of human insight in a dissolving society is one of
Robinson's major motifs. But in "Benedick" there seems to be
no real mystery, and the poem's conjectures no doubt are true.
Furthermore, the poem is full of the frank dexterity and tricki-
ness of light verse—alliterations and reiterations, conspicuous
rhymes, the wordplay of "toil" and "toils," the stylish phrasing
of "his name is also hers," and the joke about "hangings." With
few exceptions, the poems of *Guest Book* read like superior
products of a party game, and one gathers that each of them is
in fact about some specific friend or acquaintance of Bynner's;
since we cannot judge how well the subject has been hit off,
and are thus denied some of the party fun, it is surprising how
diverting some of the better poems are.

Bynner's two collections of the 1940's, *Against the Cold*
(1940) and *Take Away the Darkness* (1947), remind one by their
titles that the poet, who had symbolically died at the end of
Eden Tree, was now entering his sixties and must begin to think
about dying in earnest. *Against the Cold* is, in fact, a book of
seven sections organized (*without* any culpable "tidiness")
around the idea of death. With one exception, the sections con-
sist of a number of self-sufficient pieces which are nonetheless
significantly linked. Section I, for example, begins with rumors
and stirrings of life in winter, follows that with lyrics concerning
spring flowers and spring plowing, and then intensifies the sea-
son with the presence of a lover; yet in the very white of cherry
blossoms there comes a premonition of winter's return, and the
rest of the section sketches an estrangement which will leave
the poet older, colder, and nearer to death. All of this material
is reworked toward a different outcome in Section VII, the son-
net sequence which ends the book and gives it its title; and
between the first and last sections, in ways which it would be

laborious to tell, five classes of subject are viewed by a mind alerted to mortality. One of Bynner's weapons against the cold is humor, and the mockery of whatever is deadening; we have this at its most hilarious, here, in the poem "Episode of Decay," and the reader who is interested in the art of book arrangement may wish to note that, in the ordering of *Against the Cold*, "Episode of Decay" is immediately followed by the serious poem "Moles." Both poems are about inferior and vicious creatures who devour the lives of others, but one might not readily connect them, so different are they in tone, were they not printed side by side. So situated, they produce together a rich and angry chord.

"The Wintry Mind" may serve as an example of how, in a good little poem of his later period, Bynner could not only distribute his subject matter subtly and evenly, avoiding local obtrusions of word or figure, but could also make rhyme and meter subserve "the entirety."

> *Winter uncovers distances, I find;*
> *And so the cold and so the wintry mind*
> *Takes leaves away, till there is left behind*
> *A wide cold world. And so the heart grows blind*
> *To the earth's green motions lying warm below*
> *Field upon field, field upon field, of snow.*

The poem is based not on one scene or moment, but on the gradual alteration of a landscape, and the poet's gradual response to it. This landscape is a very sketchy one, which over a period of time loses its leaves, exposes its cold distances, and then is covered with snow; yet it seems actual and particular, because the poem speaks of the place and its weather from beginning to end, and in the last line firmly roughs-in a deep perspective of snowy fields. What we have, then, to start with, is a poem about the numbing effect of winter on mind and heart: the poet's mind partakes of the growing bleakness of the winter world, and the unreminded heart forgets that "green motions" of new life underlie the snow. If Wallace Stevens's famous poem "The Snow Man" tells how, by attunement to cold and desolation, one may achieve "a mind of winter" and thus enjoy a temporary aesthetic triumph, Bynner's "The Wintry Mind" tells how too long an attunement to winter may prove an emotional privation.

Is there more than that in this obviously simple poem? The words "I find," in the first line, look pointless if one sees no more in the poem than the poet's dealings with winter; a man need not wait until his sixties to "find" that, as the leaves fall, stark distances become visible. It helps, therefore, to remember that "The Wintry Mind" belongs in a book called *Against the Cold*, a book in which the seasons, while evoked in convincing physical detail, have also their traditional symbolism. In the light of that recollection, the first line may be seen as announcing, in the appropriate setting of winter, a discovery about approaching age. Age, the poet finds, is like winter in that it is a time of losses and of increasing loneliness—of "distances" in that sense. Furthermore, age may beget in us a "wintry mind" which, in the poem's figure, somehow collaborates with the cold in "taking leaves away." Brutally paraphrased, those words signify that an aging man may distance the world by shrinking into himself, retreating into his own thoughts, and rejecting the world about him. Between his losses and his rejections, this poem says, an old poet may live in an empty world, no longer capable of taking heart from the continuity of life.

The rhyme scheme of this pentameter poem is *ad hoc*,

"organic," and unusual, and it could have been distractingly clangorous had Bynner not muted lines 2–4 by mid-line pauses and runovers. As it is, the rhyming of *find, mind, behind,* and *blind* supports much else expressive of the poet's resignation or melancholy and the inexorability of winter and age: the repetition, for example, of "And so...and so...And so..." or the last line's "Field upon field, field upon field." Another and obvious effect of the rhyme pattern is that the first four lines, by their monotony of rhyme, strengthen the brief outburst of the earth's counter-music in line 5. A final effect of the poem's form is visual, or, as we would put it now, "concrete." In a poem which sees so broadly and so deeply, and which looks across "field upon field," there is a repeated impression of horizontality—an impression strong enough to remind this reader, at least, that "verse" derives from the Latin word for "furrow," and to make the first four lines, with their terminal sameness, suggest a level succession of barren fields. What disrupts this pattern, and in a manner supportive of Bynner's meaning, is the explosive verticality implicit in "earth's green motions."

Take Away the Darkness is a large collection which treats all of Bynner's established themes, and which he perhaps expected would be his last: it is uncommon, after all, for anyone to persist in the lyric mode for more than half a century. One sign that this book may have been imagined as a final bow is the presence in it of that café-table poem which *The Nation* had published twenty-one years before, and of a striking poem called "Circe," which, under the title "To a Dead Beauty," had appeared in *The International* for March 1914. Still, if Bynner included in the volume a few long-uncollected items, *Take Away the Darkness* is far from being a jumble of styles. Though mostly metrical and rhymed, its poems tend to have a quick naturalness of manner consonant with a readiness to be blunt and brief. The earlier Bynner may have overused words like "loveliness," or pretty phrases like "reck not a whit," or sounded archly appealing; but all that has been pretty well jettisoned here, and one result is that his political verse is now stronger both as art and as persuasion.

DEFEAT

On a train in Texas German prisoners eat
With white American soldiers, seat by seat,
While black American soldiers sit apart,
The white men eating meat, the black men heart.
Now, with that other war a century done,
Not the live North but the dead South has won,
Not yet a riven nation comes awake.
Whom are we fighting this time, for God's sake?
Mark well the token of the separate seat.
It is again ourselves whom we defeat.

Bynner's politics, the early ideological basis of which we have seen, were always both serious and *engagées*. Long before literary America became monolithically left-wing, he was an organizer or active figure in social causes. A photograph of May 6, 1911, shows him and John Dewey leading the men's contingent of a parade for woman suffrage down Fifth Avenue; and he was always an advocate of Indians and blacks. It is good to see a poem of political indignation, like the one above, which does not subvert itself by being high-flown or sanctimonious. The poem begins with the planking down of undeniable and intolerable facts, line by line, and it comes back, at the end, to a contemplation of "the separate seat" and its meaning: the general impression is of an evidential poem which says, "Look at that, and that, and that. What do you think?" Now, the poem does in fact tell us what to think, but for two reasons no flushed, hectoring poet's face interposes itself between us and the data. For one thing, the oppositions of *German* and *American*, *prisoners* and *soldiers*, *white* and *black*, *with* and *apart*, *live* and *dead*, *North* and *South*—all of which have a compelling rhetorical effect—are initially a part of the objective situation, and seem no more thrust upon us than the rocking of the train would be, had the poet mentioned it. For another thing, the bitter joke of line 4, and the ensuing recollection of the Civil War, seem the obligatory responses of anyone able to witness and remember; and when the poem threatens to sound "poetic," in line 7, Bynner end-stops the line in the middle of a couplet and follows with a colloquial outburst which might be any decent person's. Partisan political poetry usually fails, even when we sympathize with its position, either because it distorts and excludes facts or because, in the presence of some urgent human situation, it asks us to admire an emotional and artistic performance. Bynner's "Defeat" makes neither mistake.

I think of many other poems in *Take Away the Darkness* which deserve more comment than I can give. There is, for instance, "More Lovely than Antiquity," which builds up to one of those bizarre and yet apposite figures which *Spectra* had emboldened Bynner to attempt from time to time. And there is the four-line poem "Answer":

> *Cease from the asking, you receive the answer.*
> *God is not God, life life nor wonder wonder*

> *Save as a man himself becomes the dancer*
> *Across all variations of the thunder.*

Here Bynner appears to recover from the pains of uncertain identity expressed in *Eden Tree*, and to accept his restless diversity as a good thing, reaffirming to some extent what he had said in a prose "credo" written during his twenties. "Are we not many people inside ourselves? Do we not begin, compact of many ancestors? Do we not add still other lives from lovers, friends, and books? . . . Experimenting, suffering, learning with God in His growth toward that perfection which is in His blood and ours, a man becomes mankind and mankind God." If there is a notable difference between the old poet's "Answer" and the young man's "credo," it may lie in this poem's stress, not upon the loving incorporation of others, but on the full expression of the poet's many selves. Given the assumption that mankind is becoming God, and that there is nothing more divine than human self-realization, Bynner could not have found a better metaphor than the one we are offered here: man, in this poem (as also in the poem "Clouds"), usurps the thunder and lightning which were attributes of the old father-gods and turns them into a varied music and dance which express his versatile nature. The first line of the poem is reminiscent of "Find me, and turn thy back on heaven"—the paradox which concludes Emerson's "Brahma." It also reminds me of Yeats's statement that we can embody the truth but cannot know it; and I daresay that something akin to that is meant.

From his previous volumes Bynner selected *Book of Lyrics* (1955), adding to the pick of his shorter poems a handful of new efforts; and then, at the age of seventy-nine, he surprised his readers with *New Poems 1960*, a batch of 131 strange little poems which, so he declared, had come to him, during a brief period, fully verbalized in sleep. Given the poet's reputation as a hoaxer, such a claim was bound to meet with skepticism, and Bynner himself said that the *New Poems* were in some sense a harking back to *Spectra*. In what sense might that be true? The poems do not seem directed against any school of poetry then in need of debunking. They are not all of the same character, and some, like this one, are in a dreamy way quite clear and quite beautiful:

> *Barnacles on underposts of the piers*
> *Are shown under green sashes*
> *Which let elements do the dancing*
> *Round its fixed limbs*
>
> *A better ballet*
> *Than any active limbs could do*
> *Even in a forest*
> *Green with slow scarves*

Another sort of poem altogether is this subtle epigram:

> *Kindness can go too high*
> *Even in heaven*
>
> *A hawk carrying a fish*
> *For instance*
>
> *And giving it air*

Those two poems are imaginatively limber, but there is no element of travesty or crypto-badness in them, and so I think we must hunt elsewhere for the link between *New Poems* and

Spectra. Perhaps these lines from a Spectric poem, "Opus III," will indicate an answer:

> *After the end*
> *Comes always the beginning . . .*
> *And when you begin to understand this*
> *I shall have done with meaning it.*

That sort of thing and *The Beloved Stranger's* impatience with rationality ("How long must the wind go round in a mill/ And the meaning be drawn?") strike me as pointing toward what are the most frequent features of *New Poems*: non sequiturs, absurdities, logical contradictions, the "Zen" explosion of concepts. The following *may* be a poem which (like several in the book) makes entire sense, though in a crazy way:

> *Coming down the stairs*
> *She paused midway*
> *And turned*
> *And assembled the railing*
> *Which thereupon went upstairs*
> *Leaving her slowly alone*

That is, those lines may tell of a woman who is descending to join her company below, feels ill or shaken, turns, and follows the banister upstairs toward her room. Or they may mean nothing of the kind. In any event, the descriptive method makes the poem quite at home in a book full of such outright anomalies as backward-flying birds, uncast shadows, and promenading oysters.

Are we to believe Bynner's story that these witty and economical poems coalesced in his brain during the hypnopompic state, and were simply copied out upon his waking? Douglas

Day, writing in *Shenandoah* for Winter 1961, points out that the book is replete with an imagery of ocean and of sanctuary which belongs to subconscious experience, and puts also in evidence the fact that Bynner had long been attracted to the spare, direct, and concrete poetic method of China. It seems just possible to Day that Bynner had absorbed Chinese standards and practice so deeply that "his dream-visions [could] come neatly packaged out of his subconscious as *shih* poems of the T'ang Dynasty." Despite the fact that one or two poems are reminiscent of prior and conscious work, and despite the verbal and logical cleverness of some of the pieces, I too think that a possibility.

"Versatility and the willingness to try new forms," says Day elsewhere in his article, "have always been Bynner's greatest fortes." Paul Horgan likewise speaks of Bynner's "variousness" as a man, and lauds his ability to accompany "each kind of response to life with a form appropriate to it." It is certainly true that Bynner was always more venturesome and flexible than his customary assignment to the ranks of "conservative moderns" would suggest: he wrote odes, verse portraits, plays, nonsense jingles, canticles, *shih* octaves, hoax poems, propaganda pieces, visions, confessions, dream compositions, and much else. Such variety of genre and technique was good in itself; if a man is many-sided, it is well for all his sides to be articulate. But Bynner was not, in fact, at his best in every vein, and I find him most unusual not for his Protean quality but for the extent to which he invested his own poetry with Chinese qualities, succeeding so well in his most durable work that, as Day puts it, "he hardly seems to belong to any tradition that can be called American."

There are poems in *Grenstone*—"Driftwood," for example— which show a predisposition toward the aesthetic which commences to operate in *The Beloved Stranger*, fully informs the Chapala poems of *Indian Earth*, and governs much of Bynner's superior writing thereafter. To show how conscious of all this Bynner was, let me quote him once more, this time from a letter to his friend Ficke:

> I know that there is in the finest poetry of Asia a beauty far surpassing the poetry of Europe . . . but, try though I may, I apparently cannot put into English words the thing I feel—the thing that is unmistakably to be found in the work of the greater Chinese poets. English and American poetry seem to me child's-play compared with the severe beauty of the Chinese—the abstention from superfluous comment, the hard selectiveness—and, mind you, all this done in perfectly collo-quial language, which somehow achieves the beauty of frozen jade. How can we put that into the soft English tongue? It seems impossible.

The background of that, to be sure, is Bynner's struggle with the translations soon to appear as *The Jade Mountain*, but it is quite obvious what ameliorative characteristics the poet would like to inject, both by his translations and by his own original work, into "English and American poetry."

One aspect of Chinese art not stressed in the letter above is mentioned in this slight and very "Chinese" poem from *Indian Earth*:

> *A pepper-tree hangs and swings and hides the lake,*
> *And I hear the edging waves and the laughter of children.*
> *How can there be no sudden poems in my heart,*
> *Under the pepper-tree by my cool southern window?*
> *We sat here together yesterday, writing poems.*

You were in the yellow chair, I in the green chair.
And today I can think of nothing to say but this:
When I look up, the yellow chair is empty.

There is, of course, a "sudden poem" in the poet's heart, and we have just read it: the poet has set down in plain and presumably swift words the scene, the circumstances, and his state of feeling. Though based upon long discipline and rule, the kind of poem Bynner here emulates is suddenly, spontaneously executed so as to be the precise product of its moment.

Bynner was not invariably spontaneous: there is a labored jocularity, sometimes, in the texture of his *Guest Book* sonnets, and he occasionally reworked or pared down old material: for instance, a twenty-seven-line poem called "Seas and Leaves," included in *Grenstone Poems*, reappears thirty-eight years later, in *Book of Lyrics*, as an eight-line poem called "The Vessel." But it was essential to his mature theory of poetry, and usual in his practice, that any line of verse should be or seem "a moment's thought." Most serious poets whom I have known would react with incredulity to the notion of sitting about with other people, in green or yellow chairs, and "writing poems." Yet I accept the poem just quoted as fact, and I have read of Bynner's composing, in the midst of a roomful of guests at Santa Fe, verses which were later quite justifiably sent to the printer. As regards compositional "suddenness," he appears to have meant it.

Those who remember Bynner's work, whether favorably or not, always observe that he wrote too much. Indeed he did, and I am sure that one reason for the waning of his reputation was that, in his later years, he permitted so many dashed-off lines to be used as magazine filler. Having said that, I hasten to add that he was writing, much of the time, according to an aesthetic standard not shared with other poets of his caliber, or with the majority of his readers. He was, therefore, in his isolation, an uncertain judge of his own work, and was often misread. Selden Rodman, reviewing *Book of Lyrics* in *The New York Times*, praised among other qualities its "plainness of statement." Another reviewer, however, was disappointed precisely by that plainness: "It is rather surprising," he wrote, "that at the end of his life, a man so genuinely interested in poetry should not have developed a more individual style." And still another reviewer, writing in the *U.S. Quarterly Book Review*, granted the *Lyrics* their good points but asserted that "they make no great attempt toward the modification of a tradition, which is so often the mark of the great craftsmanship that is also great poetry."

It is not my purpose to prove that Bynner is thrice-great, but I will so far contradict that third reviewer as to say that much of Bynner's poetry is innovative; unfortunately, it did not innovate in an expected manner, and indeed its distinctiveness could readily be misconstrued as a deficiency. Housman congratulated Bynner on the "high level of purity and simplicity" maintained in *The Jade Mountain*, but added, "Of Chinese poems I generally feel that, while they are free from the usual vices of western poetry, they have not enough positive virtue." The densities, dimensions, and heightenings which Housman felt the want of in Chinese poetry would also seem lacking, to many Western readers, in those poems of Bynner's which somehow follow the Chinese model. I confess that I have had to adapt my taste considerably, in making this selection, so as to discern which poems are deceptively simple, which are beautifully simple, and which are too damned simple.

I said above that Bynner "did not innovate in an expected manner." Let me explain. Critics generally reserve the word "experimental" for those who continue the work of other poets deemed experimental: thus a poet of our present moment who studiously omits the vowels from the word "said," or imitates the techniques of Williams or Neruda, will be considered experimental. Rather than challenge that established usage, I shall say that Bynner turns out to have been, in the high moments of his varied career, an original poet. Hildegarde Flanner wrote in 1940: "While not an adherent to an experimental group, Mr. Bynner has advanced lyrical writing in our century through the ingenious use of traditional form. No one else has, either with satiric or serious purpose, better achieved the contrasting effects of the intense and the casual, the passionate and the nonchalant. . . ." In such work, she said, Bynner possesses what "can only be referred to as psychological velocity, a way of getting with speed and smoothness from one point to the next." One might add that Bynner did things both fine and new in forms which were not traditional, or not traditional with us. Because one does not want to see any original talent lost in the small type of explanatory footnotes, it is good to see that *The Penguin Companion to American Literature* (1971) includes a substantial entry by Malcolm Bradbury, who observes in Bynner's work "the clarity and economy of the Chinese influence" and concludes by saying: "He is a poet of real interest and considerable endurance, altering with half a century of poetic modes and fashions, yet retaining a distinctive voice." I hope that the reader of this book will agree.